GPS for Financial Christian Living

Ed Anthony

ECS
MINISTRIES
The Word to the World

GPS for Financial Christian Living

Ed Anthony

For permissions or supplements please contact:
ECS Ministries
P.O. Box 1028
Dubuque, IA 52004-1028
phone: (563) 585-2070
email: ecsorders@ecsministries.org
website: www.ecsministries.org

All Bible verses are taken from either the New Translation by J. N. Darby (JND) or the King James Version (KJV). Book and cover design by Rachel Brenneman and Maia Zaykova.

Note to the Reader:

The author has attempted to verify all information contained in this text as of the time of publication. The area of finance can change quickly. Financial instruments and laws are created and change on a daily basis. The book looks at financial issues from a biblical basis rather than the perspective of what will make the most money. The author suggests that readers seek godly, professional counsel where appropriate that will take into account their specific situation. The author does not assume any liability whatsoever for the reader's financial decisions as they are between the individual and the Lord. The biblical insights provided in the text are based on the Bible alone and do not necessarily reflect a particular tradition or denominational viewpoint. The author takes the biblical perspective and uses the generic "he" to represent an individual when the context is not gender specific.

About the Author

Ed Anthony is a Bible teacher and speaker devoted to making a difference in the lives of those he comes in contact with. As a former professor, elder, church treasurer, and financial counselor, he has many years of experience in the area of personal financial planning. Ed currently ministers as an itinerant Bible teacher at local churches around the country as the Lord leads. He is regularly invited to speak at Bible seminars, camps, and conferences throughout the United States and Canada. Originally from Connecticut, he now resides in the Nashville, Tennessee area with his wife, Barbara.

About the Book

This book focuses on the Christian and biblical perspective concerning personal financial matters. In order to keep the size of the book to a minimum much of the standard personal financial information concerning the working of various financial instruments and markets is not covered. If readers would like a complete understanding of personal financial matters, it is best that they read this book along with an industry book or text that deals with these areas. This book attempts to fill a void left by the world's books which may be quite good in understanding how things work in the physical realm of financial tools but have nothing that conveys the spiritual perspective that is important to the Christian seeking to do God's will. May the Lord receive the glory for any benefit derived from this work by His people.

GPS for Financial Christian Living

1. Acquiring the Satellite – Christ Preeminent
2. Entering the Destination – Plan
3. Detour Planning – Get Help
4. It's a Long Journey – Spend Wisely
5. Points of Interest – Live Debt Free
6. Via Point – Invest for the Future
7. Final Destination – A Faithful Steward

Contents Overview

Contents

Part Three   Stewardship Planning and the Future

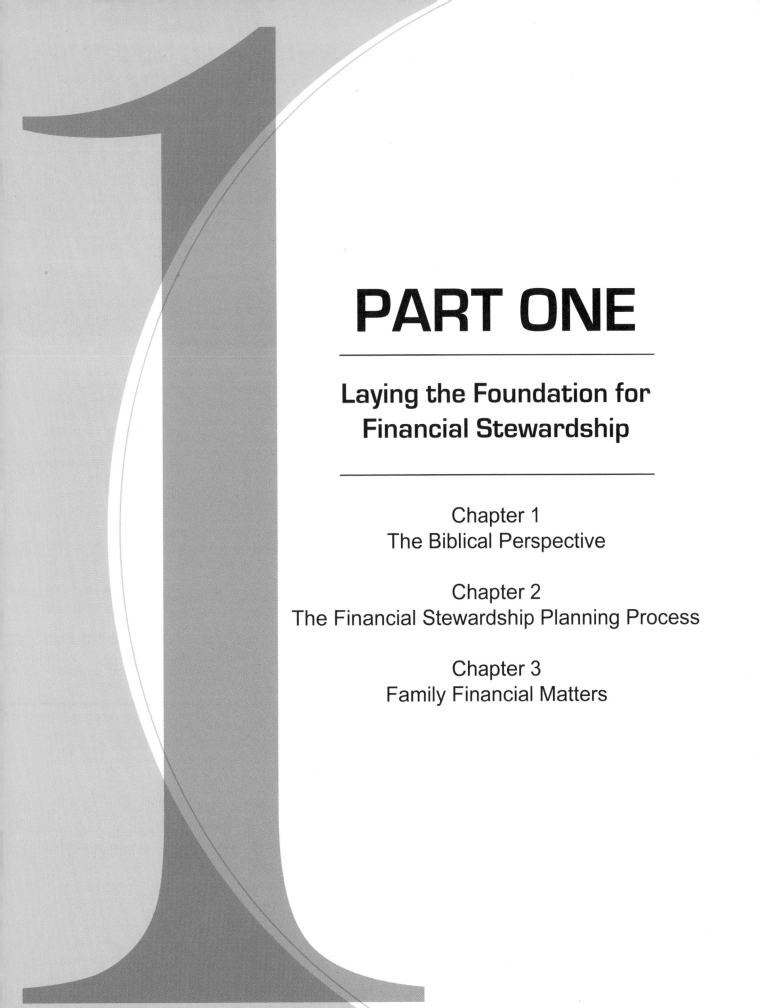

PART ONE

Laying the Foundation for Financial Stewardship

CHAPTER 1

The Biblical Perspective

Learning Objectives

1. Identify the biblical basis for financial planning and the three key factors in preparing a financial plan.

2. Explain the key differences between how the world views personal financial planning and how the Christian views it.

3. Understand from a biblical perspective what it means to be a steward of what God, as the owner of all, has given you.

4. Explain the Christian's motivation and reward for being a good steward of the Lord.

5. Describe the "counting the cost" perspective described in the Bible from both a Christian financial and discipleship view.

6. Examine and understand the three components that should influence the direction of your financial planning as a Christian.

Lord, I commit myself to you.

Lord, help me to be the steward you would want me to be. I desire to know your Son, and to know Him better, that I might walk as He walked in this world recognizing that I am just a pilgrim passing through this wilderness. May I seek, by your Spirit, to recognize how your ways are different from the world's ways. Help me to understand how to properly count the cost in all that I undertake that I, according to your will, might be blessed with all spiritual blessing in your Son. I thank you even now for what you will do in my life and with the resources you provide. As I undertake this study of biblical stewardship I commit to being a faithful steward of all that you give me according to your Word.

Getting Oriented to God

Our first section heading above clearly sets this personal financial planning book apart from others. You may be a student taking the course because it's required and so you see it as something that you must do. Perhaps you are one who has experienced the ravages of the world's insatiable desire for riches and realize there must be more to life. Whatever your situation, to gain the freedom from the world that the Bible speaks about you must understand what the Bible has to say about it. The Bible is very clear on what is needed to be able to understand it. It says: *"But we have received not the spirit of the world, but the Spirit which is of God: which also we speak, not in words taught by human wisdom but in those taught by the Spirit, communicating spiritual things by spiritual means. But the natural man does not receive the things of God, for they are folly to him; and he cannot know them because they are spiritually discerned"* (1 Corinthians 2:11-14, JND). The caveat is that one must have the Spirit of God to understand what God has to say. Without the Spirit of God within, the things of God appear as foolishness. Some of the things we will touch on together in this book are looked on as foolishness to the world because they can only be discerned or understood by the Spirit of God.

Notice that understanding comes via the Spirit of God and not by the wisdom of men. When it comes to the things of God it is the Spirit of God that enlightens us. It does not matter how many degrees whether theological, financial, or otherwise we have earned. It's not that God cannot use education or degrees, in fact, in many cases He does. Yet, when it comes to teaching the things of God, He uses men gifted by His Spirit to teach and preach what the world calls foolishness. It is interesting to note that most business or Bible schools today would not hire most of the New Testament writers or apostles because they would not have the man-made requirements to teach the things of God. Thankfully despite these things, the Spirit of God still works and can show even the most unlearned what God has to say.

This is what is great for us. No matter what our background or education God, by His Spirit, can enlighten us to how we should live our lives, and that includes being stewards of the resources we receive. Now the question that may come to mind is: How do we receive this Spirit of God so we can understand what is conveyed in the Bible about financial stewardship? Well, we can be assured that it is not difficult. In fact, the work has been done. Remember the historical facts about Jesus? Jesus came as the Son of God, as a man lived a perfect life, died, and rose again. These are historical facts that few will try to argue with. But assenting to those facts does not mean believing them. The key to receiving His Spirit within you is believing that He came and died **for you**. See, there are two paths in life, the path that leads to destruction (which by default we are

all on because of sin) and the path that leads to life. Life can be had by recognizing and believing, by faith, that Jesus Christ died for your sins and rose again by the power of God that you might have a hope. This hope is life everlasting with Him. Consider John 3:16-18. It states: *"For God so loved the world, that he gave his only-begotten Son, that whosoever believes on him may not perish, but have life eternal. For God has not sent his Son into the world that he may judge the world, but that the world may be saved through him. He that believes on him is not judged, but he that believes not has already been judged, because he has not believed on the name of the only-begotten Son of God"* (JND). Are you judged (condemned) or do you have life? The key is faith. *"But without faith it is impossible to please Him. For he that draws near to God must believe that He is and that He is a rewarder of them who seek Him out"* (Hebrews 11:6, JND). Now, if we receive Christ by faith, which is required to enter heaven, as well as understand His will for our lives, where is the Spirit that will give us understanding and wisdom that concerns God? It comes by faith in Christ. Romans 8:9-16 makes this very clear. 1 Corinthians 3:16 notes: *"Do ye not know that ye are the temple of God and that the Spirit of God dwells in you?"* Paul is pointing out that the local church at Corinth had the Spirit of God dwelling in them and that this was an indication that each believer, in the church, was indwelt by the Spirit. Romans 8:9 is emphatic concerning the connection between the believer and the indwelling Spirit: *"If any one has not the Spirit of Christ he is not of Him"* (JND).

So in simple faith, believing that Christ died for you and took on Himself your sins, you too can receive His Spirit so you can begin to understand all that He has in store for you from His Word. With that Spirit you can begin to have true understanding and wisdom that comes from above. God has changed many a life. Will you let Him change yours today?

The Preeminence of Jesus Christ

At this point we assume you know Jesus Christ as your personal Savior and as a result have been indwelt by His Spirit. With that in mind you will now be able to understand that the first key in financial planning is that Christ is preeminent in all things. The world would have us think that "We are #1" and that we need to "Look out for #1" but the Bible shows quite the contrary. All that we have we owe to what Christ has done.

Christ – the Creator and Sustainer of All

As Christians who are interested in pursuing God's will for our lives and handling our financial matters according to His insights we must first recognize fully who it is that has created all that is available to us and who keeps this world afloat (or in space for that matter). We want to first note that Christ, as one with God and uncreated, was involved in the creation of the world. Concerning Christ's involvement in all creation Paul writes, "Who is the image (not likeness) of the invisible God (God in a form we can see), firstborn (first in rank or position) of all creation (as uncreated He heads all that is created); because by Him were created all things…all things have been created by Him (implying that He has always existed) and for Him. And He is before all and all things subsist together by Him…that He might have the first place in all things" (Colossians 1:15-18, JND).

The whole book of Colossians emphasizes the preeminence and sufficiency of Jesus Christ in all things. After coming to Christ the first key lesson for us to learn concerning the world of biblical finance is that Christ must be recognized as preeminent in all things in our lives. If other things such as school, career, family, and the like are more important in your life than Christ then you will not be able to fully take advantage of the peace and freedom (John 8:36) that the Bible offers when it comes to your finances as well as other areas of your life. This is the very issue that the Lord deals with in Luke 14 where He says "If any man come to me, and shall not hate his own father and mother, and wife, and children, and brothers and sisters, yea, and his own life too, he cannot be my disciple; and whoever does not carry his own cross and come after me cannot be my disciple." (vv. 26-27, JND). This may appear to be a very harsh verse and without the Spirit of God, that is what it appears to the world. Yet, by the Spirit we can understand what this verse means. The issue is one of preeminence and place. That is, in order to put Christ first in our thinking requires us to deny that first place to others in this world. This is nearly impossible to do in the flesh but by the Spirit of God we can take up our cross and give Him His rightful place as first in our lives. Bearing the cross is often misunderstood as bearing some kind of burden but that is not the issue at all here. The issue is the preeminence of Christ by denial of the world's desired place in our lives. The cross is the instrument of death. When you take up your cross you are symbolically putting to death the world as having first place in your life.

If you truly want to have freedom and peace in this life concerning your personal finances it is imperative to put Jesus Christ first in your life. If you are unwilling to do this, your financial plans are bound to go awry because the world and its techniques will find a way to influence the flesh. The world spends millions trying to understand how the human body, mind, and emotions work so that they might create the best techniques to get you to do financially that which you really should not do. In this book we will touch on some of the things that the world does to try to influence you to make decisions that sometimes you do not even realize you are making. God has given us a marvelous mind with the ability to reason properly and weigh alternatives. Be sure to commit to putting Christ first so that you will use that mind as God intended, not only for your peace and freedom, but for Christ's glory.

Christ – the Owner and Provider of All

Now that we understand that by Jesus Christ all things were created and subsist, we can now take the next step and understand that as the Creator He in reality owns everything. If He owns everything then what we have is by His providing it. Now before you run off and stop going to school or working, we need to keep in mind how God works in providing what He owns to us for our use. For instance, we know that one of the ways God provides for us and our families is through our working in the world at various trades. This is biblical and the Bible makes it quite clear that if a man does not work, then he should not eat (2 Thessalonians 3:10). So it would seem that as long as you do not eat you do not need to work ☺. Of course, the intent of the verse is the opposite. Otherwise, not eating would lead to death. The point is clear that God desires that men acquire some of His resources through work in order to provide for their own needs in the world. This, of course, is only one way God provides, but it does illustrate that He provides by various means and some require action on our part.

That the Lord owns all is an important concept that is much different than the world's perspective. If we understand that He is the owner of all, we take a far different view of how we manage resources than if they were our own. The same would likely be true if we were to ask you to manage a million dollars while we were away for a year, especially in light of the reward we will give you for handling it well. You are likely to be much more careful about how you use those funds than you would normally be of your own. We are not saying you should not manage your own funds as well as ours but your view naturally changes when the owner changes. Interestingly, after being a steward of another's resources and seeing the possible return, you might want to handle yours much differently. 1 Corinthians 10:26 notes, "for the earth is the Lord's, and the fullness thereof." Paul is quoting the phrase from Psalms 24:1. It specifically states that "the earth is the Lord's and the fullness thereof; the world and they that dwell therein" (KJV). There are many other verses that support the fact that God is the owner of all. For further study, consider verses such as Deuteronomy 10:14; 1 Chronicles 29:11-12; Psalms 50:10-12; and Haggai 2:8.

If God is the Owner then how does He provide us with these things that He owns? We have already noted that He often can do this by our work. Paul was a tentmaker and God at least partially provided for him through that work (Acts 18:3). Ever since the fall in the Garden of Eden it appears that man receives God's provision, for the most part, through work. It appears that before the fall, the work was not as toilsome as after (Genesis 2:10, 3:19).

God does provide by means other than work. That God miraculously intervenes in the affairs of men based on His own volition and in answer to prayer is clear from scripture. That is, God does not use us as robots but allows men a sphere within which they can exercise free will. God knows the ultimate end and He has ultimate control. Although men's ways for the most part lead to evil, God's intervention is always good and just. This intervention at times includes divine judgment. Some verses to study that emphasize God's control and intervention include Psalms 135:6, Proverbs 21:1, and Acts 17:26. Sometimes God can take that which is intended for evil and use it for good as in Joseph's case (Genesis 45:4-8, 50:19-21). Of course, Christians often quote Romans 8:28 recognizing that all things work together for good to those that love God. The fact that God will provide for all our basic needs is clear as can be seen in Matthew 6:31-33 and Philippians 4:19. In fact, 1Timothy 6:8 notes that it is with these things that we should be content. God directly intervened to provide for the needs of the nation of Israel in the wilderness (and for Elijah who was fed by the ravens (1 Kings 17:4-6, KJV). The key is to seek Him first.

Besides work and direct intervention, God often provides through others for our needs. The church at Macedonia provided for others liberally (2 Corinthians 8:1-2). 1 Timothy 5:18 speaks of the church providing for widows. These same widows are those who have helped others (1 Timothy 5:10). Of course, there are many cases in the gospels where individuals ministered to the Lord Jesus.

In summary, then, God provides resources that He owns to you in one of three ways. They are by your efforts such as work or investing, by the assistance of others, and by direct intervention. The frequency that God uses these three, based on the external evidence, is in the order given.

The Christian as a Steward versus a Consumer

Have you ever noticed how often we are identified as "consumers" in the world? In fact, it appears to have become ingrained in our thinking. Even the measurement of inflation, or the increase in prices of goods, is reported by the Consumer Price Index (CPI). If we see ourselves as merely consumers then the world has us where it wants us. Have you ever considered what the term consumer means? The word comes from the root – consume, which according to Webster's dictionary means "to destroy or expend by use; use up; to eat or drink up; devour, to spend (money, time, etc.) wastefully." So a consumer is one who undertakes these things. Now, using that definition, would you want to have the constant title of being a consumer? We understand that we consume food and water to keep our bodies alive but would you use the term in general to identify your life?

The Bible takes quite a different look and emphasizes that we are stewards rather than consumers. Stewardship involves not only using up some resources but developing and making others grow as well. Over a period of time the result of their use leaves something of greater worth than when you started. Webster's defines a steward as "one who manages another's property or financial affairs; one who administers anything as the agent of another or other." This is the biblical view of who you are as a Christian. There are many examples dealing with stewards and stewardship in the Bible. For study look at Joseph as a steward in Potiphar's house (Genesis 39:1-4) and later in the land of Egypt (Genesis 41:39-44); the parable of the stewards in Matthew 25:14-29; the parable of the wise steward in Luke 12:42-44; and how the elders must demonstrate good stewardship of what God has given them (Titus 1:7).

The property is not always money as can be seen in Titus but whatever the Lord provides. There are some other key things to notice as well. God recognizes that there are differing levels of skill and talent in each individual. For instance, in Matthew 25 one was given five talents, one was given two, and the last given one talent. Have you ever noticed what he says to the first two concerning what they received in the first place? The issue was not who was more talented or had more abilities or gifts, but their faithfulness to use what the Lord gave. Although the sums that were given to the first two stewards were different, the Lord calls both sums "a few things." Both were commended in the same way because the result (a 100% growth of the resource) was the same. The Lord knows the steward and He only desires that we be faithful in the little He has given us here on earth. Notice also that the property belonged to their lord just as what we have belongs to our Lord.

We are taught in Scripture to be good stewards, not good consumers. The world makes a significant effort to get you to use your resources as quickly as possible. This is true even if it means more waste so that you will spend more or need to purchase again. Just look at the efforts of merchants, advertisers, and creditors and you can see that it appears that they are acting in unison to help you destroy the resources rather than grow them. The Bible says it best in 1 Corinthians 4:2 – "Here, further, it is sought in stewards that a man be found faithful" (JND). In this book we will see how we can be faithful stewards of what the Lord has given and thus be able to give a good account. A consumer has nothing to show for his consumption but the faithful steward has much to show for his stewardship.

Interestingly our word economy comes from the same Greek word for steward. There is little doubt that the reader has heard

"Here, further, it is sought in stewards that a man be found faithful." 1 Cor. 4:2

about the "economy" and whether it is doing well or in recession. Today the economies of countries are much more intertwined and as a result a decline in one country may lead to a decline in other individual economies or an overall decline in the "global economy."

What is an economy? The word comes from the Greek and the word is used at least 20 times in the Bible. Economy comes from the Greek word οικονομος (oikonomos). It is composed of two parts and two roots: οικος – meaning house or household and νεμω (nemō) which means to arrange (nomos – law also comes from this; the law being an arrangement of things). This should jog your mind as that is the definition of stewardship we had seen in Webster's dictionary earlier. So, the Greek term "economy" when translated into English is "stewardship" which means to arrange a household. Thus, the idea of a system used to manage a house or household. In the Bible the term is sometimes translated "dispensation" or "administration." We will note here that "economics" is basically the study of stewardship or economic systems. If we look at the terms from the New Testament we can get a pretty good idea of what an economy is.

The various forms of the word as used in the New Testament:

The verb oikonomeō (1) – Luke 16:2 – to be a steward

The noun oikonomos (10) – Luke 12:42; 16:1, 3, 8; Romans 16:23; 1 Corinthians 4:1, 2; Galatians 4:2; Titus 1:7; 1 Peter 4:10 – steward or manager

The noun oikonomia (9) – Luke 16:2, 3, 4; 1 Corinthians 9:17; Ephesians 1:10, 3:2, 9; Colossians 1:25; 1 Timothy 1:4 – stewardship, administration, dispensation

As a result of looking at these passages we see several key characteristics that would help us to understand the idea of stewardship or an economy.

1. There are those who set the policies or laws of how the house or system is to function – for example the master or lord of the house (Luke 12:42; 16:1-8).

2. There are those who are responsible to carry out the wishes of the master (Luke 12:42, 16:1-8; 1 Corinthians 4:2; Romans 16:23).

3. There are the responsibilities or duties to be accomplished for the proper functioning of the home or system (Luke 16:1-8; 1 Corinthians 4:1).

4. There is an accountability structure in place to make sure that the system or house runs as planned (Luke 16:2).

5. There may be a change of the steward if the house does not function according to the duties and policies set by the lord of the house (Luke 16:2, 4).

6. Men are ultimately responsible to God for the stewardship they have been given (1 Corinthians 4:1; Titus 1:7).

7. Responsibilities committed by God to man must be discharged faithfully (1 Corinthians 4:2).

8. An economy or stewardship may end because the lord is changing the responsibilities or duties expected (Galatians 4:2).

9. A stewardship or economy does not need to be financial but may represent something else that God desires man to manage responsibly such as the mysteries of God (1 Corinthians 4:1; Ephesians 1:10, 3:2, 9; Colossians 1:25; 1 Timothy 1:4; 1 Peter 4:10)

Since stewardship and economy come from the same Greek word we can define either word, biblically, as an administration or management of another's property (physical or spiritual) requiring the administrator or manager to be responsible, accountable, and faithful.

Among several definitions, Merriam-Webster notes that an economy is "the arrangement or mode of operation of something: organization; a system especially of interaction and exchange."

With this new found knowledge we can see that today an economy, though more complex, really has the same characteristics as used originally. It a system that is arranged to manage resources and operate in such a way as to facilitate interaction and exchange that meets the responsibilities as defined by the owner of the system.

The Love of Christ versus the Love of Money

Perhaps you have heard the adage "money is the root of all evil." Many Christians have learned that this is not what the Bible says. 1 Timothy 6:10 notes that "the love of money is the root of every evil…" As perhaps you know, money is not the issue, but the love of it. It all comes down to coveting or desiring that which you do not have. The world says not only to look out for oneself, but that it is a great desire to be rich and have the best. Again the world is at odds with the Bible. As we have already noted the verse preceding verse ten notes that "those desiring to be rich fall into temptation and a snare, and many unwise and hurtful lusts which plunge man into destruction and ruin." Verse ten finishes with, "which some having aspired after, have wandered from the faith, and pierced themselves with many sorrows." Yet, this is exactly the way the world wants us to think so that our desires and dreams can be fulfilled.

The Bible would rather that you seek after the things of Christ. In verse 11 of this same section Paul writes "But thou, O man of God, flee these things, and pursue righteousness, piety, faith, love, endurance, meekness of spirit" (JND). Now, we realize that may not sound all that exciting to some of the young people reading this text. But if you truly know Christ and desire to serve Him this should at least tug at your heart so that you have an interest in pursuing the things of Christ which have eternal value. We need to keep in mind that we do not own anything, it is the Lord's. If it is the Lord's, then we need to keep in mind that He will ask: What have you done with it? What is the return?

If we follow the biblical perspective we could lose all our physical possessions tomorrow and still have peace and freedom in Christ because the return is more than the growth of financial resources as we have already noted. But, from the world's perspective of becoming rich, if we lost it all tomorrow we would be living in fear because we have lost what we had owned. When we recognize He is the owner we recognize His right to take it back as well, and still find peace. Job recognized this when he said "the Lord gave and the Lord hath taken away, blessed be the name of the Lord" (Job 1:21, KJV). Job recognized all that he had belonged to the Lord and even in such a loss his heart was right. Would we be able to do the same? We can, if we recognize our love must be focused on Christ and not on the mammon of this world. As the Bible notes, you can only serve one master, and it should be God (Matthew 6:24; Luke 16:13).

As young people, you will be pressed to seek after the riches of the world. Allow the Spirit of God to help you restrain the flesh that would succumb to its enticements. Paul says concerning all others but Timothy, "for all seek their own things, not the things of Christ" (Philippians 2:21, JND). Will we be counted, like Timothy, as those who truly seek the things of Christ?

The Wisdom of God versus the Wisdom of Men

The final key in dealing with the preeminence of Christ deals with our ability to reason about financial things. It is another area in which the Bible has something significant to say. When looking at financial issues we may be inundated by help from the world. We can be assured that the world's true desire is to relieve you of some of your funds or resources. In a later section, on the plan of the Christian, we will detail the three resources that

will be of importance to you in making the right decisions (assuming that you have decided to make Christ preeminent).

The world's mechanisms are not always, and perhaps we should say rarely, the mechanisms of God. The world composed of unbelievers, views things from a perspective of self and "what is in it for me." As a result, the unbeliever's thinking emphasizes schemes that enrich themselves. Do we need to go into the obvious greed that has overtaken many in the corporate world to make the point? Whether WorldCom, Enron, or some other smaller firm the façade may be to help the "consumer" but the heart is really with the money. We have already noted that our affections should not be on the mammon of the world, for who can serve two masters? The same is true of the world's wisdom. That is, the wisdom of God seems as foolishness to men since they have a different master (1 Corinthians 1:25, 2:14) and the wisdom of the world is seen as foolishness to God (1 Corinthians 3:19). If our master is Christ then our view of the way we should do things will be different. Keep in mind wisdom from a biblical perspective is more than just knowledge and understanding. Knowledge involves knowing the facts. Understanding involves using that knowledge or being able to synthesize various known facts and previous experience and weigh possible alternatives. Wisdom not only involves weighing the alternatives but making the right decisions or taking the right path.

"The love of money is the root of every evil." -1 Timothy 6:10

The question may then be raised as to whether we should use our minds. The answer is a resounding YES! The key is that the mind must be used as guided by the Spirit of God. "For let this mind be in you which was also in Christ Jesus that who subsisting in the form of God did not esteem it as an object of rapine (to be coveted) to be on an equality with God but emptied himself, taking a bondman's form, taking his place in the likeness (not image) of men" (Philippians 2:5-7, JND). Read Ephesians 4:17-24 and see if you can identify how the important the mind is. In verse 17, it notes that we should not walk as the rest of the nations walk, in the vanity of their mind that is corrupt but to, as verse 23 notes, be renewed in the spirit of our mind. The mind is a powerful thing that can do great things for God's glory when used by the Spirit of God, but it can also be extremely corrupt as can be evidenced by what we see in the world today.

You do not have to go far to see the world's desires. As the author was originally writing this chapter his wife stopped by to let him know what she had just heard on an investment show. The story is of a 71-year-old woman who thought an insurance agent (who had been

Luke 12:15

a friend of her late husband) was helping her by setting up a 17 year annuity for her. What she did not realize was that to receive any money out of the annuity required a 25% payment of the funds withdrawn. Although we do not know all the details of this transaction it became quite clear where this agent's mind was and it was not about helping the woman but helping himself to her money or to a good portion of her needed funds. Basically she would lose 25% of the annuity, meaning that she would be losing money on the investment. This is an example of the wisdom of men crafting something that is corrupt and of the flesh. We are pleased to note that there was a happy ending for this story since she had called this investment show and the man eventually went to the president of the insurance company to get it straight. Even though it was legal, the president recognized right away that it was not right and worked with the woman to get it straightened out. How many others, though, never have that happy ending, because of the covetousness of the mind and not being guided by the Spirit of God?

As we begin to delve into the details of financial planning here and in your other studies, please pray for guidance from God by His Spirit to do that which is right rather than that which is expedient in satisfying some desire. It may not be easy, especially if you are a young person in high school or college with many dreams. Be sure they are dreams that God has for you as well.

Blessing and Reward

The question will likely arise as to what the result will be if we are obedient to the Word of the Lord and are good stewards who give an account of what we have done. No doubt, there are a variety of teachings concerning this topic by various Bible teachers and churches. Some may claim that God wants all Christians to be rich while others will claim that we should give away all that we have to the poor. In this section we explore what it is that should motivate the Christian to be successful in financial stewardship and what he should expect to gain as a result.

The Christian's Motivation

Should the Christian's motivation to be a good steward be the world's riches? Some would suggest that this is the view that the Bible takes. Many verses could be used in support of such a view. Here are few examples that one might use:

There is he that scattereth, and yet increaseth; and there is he that withholdeth more than is fitting but tendeth to poverty. The liberal soul shall be made fat, and he that watereth shall be watered also himself (Proverbs 11:24-5).

But this I say, he which soweth sparingly shall reap also sparingly; and he which soweth bountifully shall reap also bountifully (2 Corinthians 9:6).

And the Lord shall guide thee continually, and satisfy thy soul in drought, and make fat thy bones; and thou shalt be like a watered garden, and like a spring of water, whose waters fail not (Isaiah 58:11).

And it shall come to pass, if thou shalt hearken diligently unto the voice of the Lord thy God, to observe and do all his commandments which I command thee this day, that the Lord will set thee on high above all nations of earth; and all these blessings shall come on thee, and overtake thee, if thou shalt hearken unto the voice of the Lord thy God. Blessed shalt thou be in the city…in the field…the fruit of thy body…the fruit of the ground…and blessed shalt thou be when thou comest in, and blessed shalt thou be when thou goest out (Deuteronomy 28:1-6).

Verses, similar to those listed, could be multiplied for many pages. The general idea being that those who are obedient to His Word or are generous in giving will be bountifully blessed. Yet one could also select a variety of verses that note that being rich is not good or being poor is a blessing:

For what is a man profited, if he shall gain the whole world, and lose his own soul or what shall a man give in exchange for his soul (Matthew 16:26)?

Blessed are the poor in spirit; for theirs is the kingdom of heaven (Matthew 5:3).

Take heed, and beware of covetousness: for a man's life consisteth not in the abundance of the things which he posseseth (Luke 12:15).

Labor not to be rich, cease from thine own wisdom (Proverbs 23:4).

Then there are other verses that that seem to take the middle road between poverty and wealth:

A faithful man shall abound with blessings, but he that maketh haste to be rich shall not be innocent (Proverbs 28:20).

Remove far from me vanity and lies, give me neither poverty nor riches; feed me with food convenient for me, lest I be full, and deny thee, and say, Who is the Lord? Or lest I be poor, and steal, and take the name of my God in vain (Proverbs 30:8-9).

As the reader can see from these verses the discussion can get quite lively in truly deciding what God has for the Christian. The answer is more difficult unless one has an understanding of the Bible as a whole. Since space precludes undertaking that kind of study we will at least note a few salient points for the reader's consideration:

1. Be careful to find who is being spoken to in the verse. Promises to Israel, for instance, may not be promises to the Christian.

2. In a similar vein, see if promises to Israel have a spiritual counterpart in the New Testament for the Christian (such as the blessing of Ephesians 1:3).

3. Does the verse in some way modify the action? For instance in Proverbs 28:20, the phrase "maketh haste" that modifies "to be rich" gives an important indication concerning the motivation of the individual.

4. Look at the context of the verses. For instance, a study of the context of the verses from Isaiah 58 above show that the portion deals with various encouragements to Israel in light of what has come before in the book. This does not mean that we should dismiss the possibility that there are still lessons for the Christian to be learned.

5. Look at the concept in relation to the whole Bible. A study of poverty and riches will show that there were many faithful believers who appeared poor (Mary and Joseph, the widow who gave her two mites, and the woman with the issue of blood, to name a few) and yet there were others who were quite rich (Joseph of Aramathea, Boaz, and Abraham to name a few). At a minimum, in each case, the issue of a right motivation is seen.

6. A proper understanding of biblical giving is important in understanding the rewards and blessings of the Christian. On the surface some verses equate giving with blessing and that the more you give the more you receive. There is of course a sense in which this is true but looking at it from a strictly physical viewpoint for the Christian leads to improper conclusions. See the chapter later in the text on giving for additional insights.

No doubt there is much more that could be said, but some of the thoughts in this section should at least help in framing the reader's thoughts and any discussion concerning the topic.

We must keep in mind that God is in control and the way He works with one person may be substantially different than another. It should be noted that one who lives in physical poverty can have as much peace and freedom as one who lives in great wealth because it is not the material things that make the difference to either. They both have spiritual riches that go far beyond the physical. This is something very important for the Christian to understand. Some Christians have pained themselves through with many sorrows thinking that God wants them to be physically rich in this present age. 1 Timothy 6:9 notes: "But those that desire to be rich fall into temptation and a snare, and many unwise and hurtful lusts, which plunge men into destruction and ruin" (JND).

Thus, the motivation for the Christian is not to be rich or poor but glorify God in his stewardship of what God provides. For ye are bought with a price, therefore glorify God in your body, and in your spirit, which are God's (1 Corinthians 6:20). We are to use our bodies not for our own pleasure and gain but for God's glory and gain. Remember it's the return for the Master that we will give an account for. Will we be ready to give a good account?

What is the Christian's Reward?

Is there any reward for the Christian who is faithful in the stewardship of what God provides? Many Christians have taken what was meant for literal Israel as true for the Christian. As a result many have made a shipwreck of their faith. Faith by its nature deals with that which cannot be seen. For Abraham and Israel faithfulness was rewarded with physical wealth and blessing. That is quite clear from the Old Testament. As a result when some do not see great physical blessing in their lives they begin to waver in their faith. But when we get to the epistles the teaching concerns the Christians and the church and the emphasis is on the spiritual blessings. The obedient faith of a Christian leads to an abundance of spiritual rather than physical blessing. Now God may see fit to abundantly bless physically as well, as He has done with many Christians but a lack of physical wealth is not an indication of a lack of obedience nor is wealth an indication of obedience. That is a view of man, not of God. It is quite evident that there are many rich in this world who know not the Lord Jesus Christ. Man looks on the outward appearance but God looks at the heart (1 Samuel 16:7). The Christian's blessing is being with Him right now. This is why Paul notes in Colossians 3:1-4 where our affections are. They are where Christ is. If that's the case then physical wealth certainly cannot be a guide for the Christian as to whether he is blessed of God. Elsewhere Paul says: "Blessed be the God and Father of our Lord Jesus Christ, who has blessed us with every spiritual blessing in the heavenlies in Christ" (Ephesians 1:3, JND). There is no

"For ye are bought with a price, therefore glorify God in your body, and in your spirit which are Gods." 1 Cor. 6:20

...at the Christian is blessed but it's always seen ...l and in the heavenlies.

...and freedom in your personal finances will come ...izing that wealth in this world does not determine whether God has blessed you. The question may then arise why be a good steward? The issue is future reward. Our stewardship here will be reflected by what we gain as a future reward in heaven and in His kingdom. Our desire is to use the resources and talents the Lord has given us on account to build "the account." That way we can look forward to giving an account as was apparently the case with two of the stewards in Matthew 25:14-29. Those who have life desire to give a good account of what is in the Master's account at the end of their lives. This account focuses on three areas including: family, where we expend resources in return for maintaining and growing lives of service to Him; ministry, where we use resources to further His work; and wealth that is saved for future uses and an inheritance. Paul speaks of the "account" in Philippians 4:17 and Romans 14:12 notes that each man will give an account. The key reminder of this accounting for the Christian, though, comes in 1 Corinthians 3:11-15 where the issue is not salvation but the work. That is, the results of the use of resources given to him will be tested by fire to determine if a reward is to be given. Faithfulness in stewardship will lead to greater reward as seen in the parable of the steward in Matthew 25.

The Plan of the Christian

Understanding God's involvement with man is important because it helps us to see that He expects us to use our minds and wills to glorify Him. The key is to be sure that the Holy Spirit is having an influence on these. With the influence of the Spirit in the life the correct decisions can be made. If only it were that easy. As you know even if you are a Christian you do not always do as you should. Basically we are doing one of two things when we do not allow God through His Spirit to have the rightful place in our lives: we either grieve or quench the Spirit. When we grieve the Spirit we basically do that which the Spirit is telling us not to do. To quench the Spirit is not to do that which the Spirit suggests to do. The first issue of grieving the Spirit occurs in Ephesians 4:30. The context describes the things that occur when you let Satan or the flesh have influence in the life. This of course is not what the Spirit desires for your life and so He is grieved when you partake of these very things. The issue of quenching the Spirit occurs in 1 Thessalonians 5:19. The context of this verse is dealing with positive things such as rejoicing, praying, and holding fast. These are the things that the Spirit certainly would have us do and if we do not He is then quenched. The leading of the Spirit is reduced or put out like a fire.

The Conscience of the Christian

Conscience as used in the New Testament means literally "a knowing with." Thus, the idea is of co-knowledge with oneself. It is a faculty that God has given us by which we can apprehend His will. Thus, our conscience will testify to us of the reality of our conduct (2 Corinthians 1:12). Hebrews 10:2 notes that the conscience makes us aware of our sin and guiltiness before God.

Our conscience judges our own actions based on what God has shown us. Thus, in 1 Corinthians 10 Paul emphasizes that understanding plays a key role in conscience judging properly (in this case regarding meat sacrificed to idols). Of course he also notes that another's conscience may not be assisted by the same level of knowledge. Thus, the result is there will be different judgments concerning the same thing by brothers and sisters in Christ. The difference in judgment usually results from incomplete knowledge being supplied to the conscience. This is why the study of God's Word in relation to our conduct in the world is so important.

With these thoughts in mind when we come to financial stewardship issues and the use of various financial instruments in the world we will no doubt encounter different judgments in some areas based on the varying levels of understanding that individuals have from God and the study of His Word. It is important to note that not all brothers and sisters in Christ will necessarily agree with all that is said in this text regarding financial issues and instruments. We leave these differences between the individual and the Lord. We believe that in these areas conscience plays an important role and we do not want to cause another brother or sister to stumble (1 Corinthians 8:9).

To be able to better judge these things and strengthen the conscience, all should seek to study God's Word to gain the knowledge that can help to make right judgments a reality. The Spirit of God will help to bring the knowledge and understanding necessary for the Christian.

Your Time in Financial Matters

As we begin to move forward in learning about financial planning and how God works with us in this world we should note briefly that "time" plays an important role as well in being a good steward. We will need to set time aside in order to perform the appropriate activities that are required of a faithful steward. Trying to be a steward on just a "time available" basis is not likely to work since there will always be more activity than time in life.

We would then recommend that specific time be set aside for reviewing budget items, setting and reviewing goals, paying bills, praying about financial issues, and the like. This should be done on a regularly basis, perhaps once every week, but whatever works best for you and your family. Remember it should be scheduled otherwise it will not get done in an organized manner.

We should also note here that though we want to set time aside to work on financial planning we do not want to be consumed by it. You could fill every waking moment working on financial issues in reading, doing research, finding the best deals, and the like. Being a good steward will take time because you want to give a good account and keep good records. There are many in the world that will spend nearly all their discretionary time consumed with making money and getting the best deals. Do not become enamored with the world's goods and "making money." Those who focus 10-20 hours a week on the world's financial system can find ways to use credit cards, loans, and other financial instruments to make money. Few people have this kind of time. We do not cover this approach in this text because of the emphasis on trying to get rich, the possibility of getting in debt, and the inordinate amount of time that would be required to keep track of finances.

In summary, then be prepared to set some time aside each week to deal with stewardship related issues. By doing this you will have time to develop appropriate financial plans as guided by the Spirit.

Your Plan – God's Direction

The next logical question that you then might ask is how do we really know if the Spirit would or would not have us do something from a financial perspective? We will get to that later in this section but we want to first recognize and discuss the fact that based on how God works among men our wills have a substantial role. As a result, God expects us to think, plan, judge, and do. This is certainly true of us as we begin our journey into understanding what God has to say about personal finances. If God is working in our lives we may well do the planning but it is God by the Holy Spirit that does the directing. This is brought out in Proverbs 16:9 which notes "A man's heart deviseth his way, but the Lord directeth his steps" (KJV). God allows us to do the planning but He wants our planning to have direction from Him so that the steps

we take are within His will. This does not mean that God does not give us options to choose from. If you are looking to buy a home and you find four that meet your needs and any of them would fit within your budget, is God going to be upset because you chose the one with the brown wood exterior because you happen to like that style? Not likely. God has given us a mind and a will to make appropriate choices. We make choices every day dealing with what we will eat, what we will wear, and what we will do for the day. Does this mean that God cannot use your choices to your and others' benefit? Does this mean that God cannot work miraculously using appropriate choices you have made? Of course not. Once we have established that we are Christians willing to be led by His Spirit we can begin the journey to financial freedom and peace. The first step in the plan is to recognize that your part is vital. Financial plans do not grow on trees nor are they one size fits all. We must make the effort to come up with a plan. The old business adage is quite applicable here: "Plan or be planned for." If you do not plan with God's leading then the world has a plan for you which usually involves relieving you of all that you receive. Make a commitment to plan today.

You as Steward and God as Owner — Accountability

We have already noted that we are called to be stewards and not consumers. We learned an important truth from 1 Corinthians 4:2 – "Here, further, it is sought in stewards that a man be found faithful." That is, stewardship is about faithfulness. We also learned that there is a unique relationship of the steward to the resources he has – they belong to another. We earlier emphasized that their owner is Christ. The goal of the steward is to earn a return on the Master's resources and we identified that there were three major areas that encompass the accounting of the stewardship. They were the family, the ministry, and the estate that is left.

In this section we want to explore the importance of the accountability as a steward. If we do not understand there is accountability then, unfortunately, the resources will likely be squandered. Accountable means having to give a report of your work. What if your professor at the beginning of the semester gave all the assignments and readings that were to be done throughout the semester and trusts that you will do them? The professor mentions that he will not be collecting the work or reviewing the things that you read. You get an A by just coming to class once in a while!! Now, after the hallelujahs die down we have this question. How many of you will have completed all the assignments and readings that the professor assigned at the beginning of the semester? Based on our experience there would be few that have. What if the professor said there would be one exam based on the assignments and readings given sometime the last 3 weeks of the semester and that would count for your entire grade? Experience again shows that most will attempt to complete most of the assignments and readings. When there is no accountability for what needs to be done our natural mind may quickly dismiss the relevance of doing all the work without considering the possible benefits that are lost by not doing it.

This all gets back to using our minds as guided by the Spirit. If you believe that God has allowed you access to a college education then you would want to be a good steward of that which is provided by that education. Yet, it never ceases to amaze us how many students, many very well intentioned, lose focus on the stewardship of their education and do not receive nearly the return that they should on it. Invariably it is accountability that determines the return on your education. Those who are dedicated to receiving the most out of their education usually are being held accountable in some way. Perhaps it is mom and dad who are paying for college, or a scholarship committee, or an employer. The key is, as stewards, they are accountable and of course you are accountable as well.

So, another important thing to understand is that as stewards we are accountable to the Master for what He provides us. Faithfulness involves accountability. How we use our resources is important and we want to be able to look forward to giving an account. In Luke 16 is the well known story of the unjust steward (1-13). There is much to be learned from this parable about finances and especially financial stewardship. In the first verse the steward of a rich man is accused of wasting the master's goods. This turned out to be true. The steward was really being a "consumer" of the master's goods and not a steward. In verse two the master appropriately requests of the steward an accounting: "give an account of thy stewardship." Literally he is to give a reckoning. Now, the steward is in a real pickle, as we might say, because he can no longer have the stewardship and yet he is quite used to living the high life. As a result he is unwilling or unable to work and too ashamed to humble himself and beg. Before we continue we see some very important truths for ourselves. We are handling the Master's goods so always keep in mind that you will be called to give an account of your stewardship of those goods. Never waste the Master's goods as a consumer as this steward did. Never put yourself in this type of situation.

Notice that the master does not bail him out by giving him more goods. As a steward you must be faithful in a little to be faithful in much (Luke 16:10). So what is the steward to do? Interestingly, you would think that the steward lacked intelligence to get himself into this mess but the steward actually was quite intelligent as can be seen by his plan for after he loses the stewardship. He basically strikes deals with all those who are debtors to his lord for less than what they owe so that when he gives the actual account to the lord and is put out of the stewardship he will have many friends in these debtors to help him out. It's sad to see that the steward did not use his intelligence in the first place.

Perhaps you know the rest of the story; the master commends the steward for his wise plan in taking care of himself. The Lord in using this parable was not condoning the dishonesty of the steward for He actually is the one that calls him "unjust." It is the master in the story that commends the steward. The purpose of the parable was to show the importance of using present opportunities for future blessing. The children of the world, whose god is mammon, seem at times to be wiser than those who are not of the world. Here the unjust steward was wise in using his present opportunity to ensure his own future blessing. We need to take hold of the present opportunities that God has given us to be a steward of what He has given that we might look forward to giving an account. As we have noted before, our blessings are for the most part spiritual, and many are future. But are we using present opportunities, financial and otherwise, to prepare for that future? 1 Peter 4:10 makes clear that these resources are more than physical but include our spiritual gifts that God has given. Luke 16:12 emphasizes that on earth we are stewards of another's things but in the future of our own. But if you have not been faithful in another's then you certainly will not be faithful with your own that would be given you at the Bema (2 Corinthians 5:10). Of course, it all comes back to whom we give the preeminence. That is the point of Luke 12:31-34. Seek first the kingdom of God – that will show where your treasure is and your heart as well. You will then look forward to giving an account of all that God has given. Luke 12:42-43 states, "And the Lord said, who is that faithful and prudent steward whom his lord will set over his household, to give the measure of corn in due season? Blessed is the bondman whom his lord on coming shall find doing thus" (JND).

Planning and Counting the Cost

In the coming chapters we discuss in detail the biblical perspective involved in financial planning and creating a plan. In this chapter we are continuing to lay the foundation so that you will be successful in the undertaking. Another important biblical truth related to planning is that it involves intelligently counting the cost. When the Lord explained that discipleship required taking up our own cross He was emphasizing that it meant putting to death or denying the world as having the first priority. He explained this concept using several parables that deal with counting the cost. These same truths dealing with discipleship apply to us as financial stewards.

The parables come from Luke 14. The first concerns the building of a tower (vv. 28-30) and the second with determining whether to go to war (vv. 31-32). In each case the Lord is trying

"Plan or be planned for."

to point out that to be His disciple requires a cost – He becomes preeminent. Likewise when making a decision we must plan and count the cost. A lack of planning means you may start out strong but run out of funds and have a building half completed. The sad part is not just the ridicule of others for your state but the likelihood that another will receive all that went into the project. This is what happened in the late eighties and again in the last few years when the real estate market had a "major correction" as some might call it. Many buildings went unfinished and were auctioned off in bankruptcy proceedings, the original owners receiving nothing after all they had put into it. Most, if not all, had not counted the cost or if they did, used a wrong perspective in counting the cost.

Planning means doing more than writing down a few things you would like to do. It means understanding how to properly calculate the cost. You do not need to be a mathematician or an engineer but you must be willing to take the time to count the cost. The world would rather you not count the cost of your decisions. That is why the world's emphasis is on getting you to buy now before it's too late. Research shows that those who take time to consider the cost of a deal do not normally take it. The merchants and advertisers know this and you need to be aware of it as well. Do any of these sound familiar? Time is limited! Call today, space is limited! This deal is only good today! Be one of the first 15 callers! And that's not all; if you order in the next 15 minutes you will receive…! They contradict the biblical perspective of counting the cost. Taking advantage of those offers lacks planning. The Bible tells us to plan and count the cost. We need to disregard that which would violate that rule. Any deal of the world that sounds too good to be true likely is too good to be true. That is, there is more than meets the eye. You will learn a great deal in this book on how to count the cost and you should find it a great benefit to you as you seek to be a good steward of the Lord.

Setting and Implementing Financial Plans

We can now summarize by saying that God expects the Christian to plan and implement financial plans as a good steward. This involves making Christ preeminent and pondering carefully using the mind that God has given us. We sometimes call this the combination of seeking and thinking. There is one last component to setting in place and implementing successful personal financial plans. We call it the doing or performance phase. See, we need all three parts: preeminence, pondering, and performance or in the vernacular; seeking, thinking, and doing. Leave any part out and our plans will fail.

That brings us to performance or doing. In order to have a plan or to make a plan of any use requires doing something. But that brings us back to the question we posed earlier that we promised to get back to. How do we really know if the Spirit would or would not have us

do something from a financial perspective? We suggest that there are three mechanisms by which we may know the mind of God concerning a matter. These can only have instrumentality if it is the Spirit of God providing the insight. That is, these three mechanisms are based on the power of the Holy Spirit. They are the Bible, prayer, and godly counsel.

We should be able to see by this point that the Bible has a great deal to say about financial matters and, in fact, it is the author's understanding from another that it is the second most touched on topic in the Bible, next to love. Although we have not confirmed this point we would certainly not be surprised. A great deal of our time is spent in stewardship type activities (working, shopping, selling, investing, etc.). It's no accident that many of the parables of the Lord used money or riches to teach a lesson. If the use of resources was so important to God to include so much in the Bible it would seem to behoove us to use it as a source for counsel and wisdom in this very area. Paul, in writing to Timothy, noted that "every scripture is divinely inspired, and profitable for teaching, for conviction, for correction, for instruction in righteousness; that the man of God may be complete, fully fitted to every good work" (2 Timothy 3:16-17, JND). These two verses say it all concerning the applicability of the Bible in determining and implementing our financial plans. Do we wish to be a fully fitted and complete steward of God? Then use His Word. There is no better source of wise counsel in this world today. Throughout this book we will draw on the truths of the Word to help us understand the direction we should take when it comes to our financial planning.

In addition to the Word as a guide, there is prayer. God communicates to us through His Word and we communicate to God through prayer. Prayer serves several purposes. Perhaps first and foremost it keeps us in fellowship with and thinking about Him. It's like the accountability of stewardship, if we are not vigilant we soon lose track of things and begin to wander off the path. The same is true with prayer. There are many examples of prayer in the Bible but in summary they fall into four key areas. They are worship (adoration) because of who He is, confession, thanksgiving for what He has done, and supplication and requests of Him. This is not a treatise on prayer so we will not go into too much detail, except to say, that all of these are an important part pf prayer. We want to emphasize that God certainly wants us to pray and it is one way by which we gain knowledge of what He would like us to do. The Word says, "the fervent supplication of the righteous man has much power (James 5:16, JND). Again we will not go into all the details of prayer but reading His Word helps us understand how and what to pray for. Praying that the Lord make us multi-millionaires will not be answered in the affirmative since it is clear that this is a wrong desire. It will seem as if the Lord is not answering since you have requested an answer to prayer that He has already given you in His Word. No better verse makes this clear than

James 4:3, "Ye ask, and receive not, because ye ask evilly (amiss), that ye may consume it in your pleasures" (JND).

The opposite of asking amiss of course is asking rightly, in faith knowing that whatever God answers is best for you. The Scripture states "if ye shall ask anything in my name, I will do it" (John 14:14, JND). Now this is where we go astray. We see the "ask anything" and right away think God will give every desire of our heart. But as we have already noted, the Bible also notes that we can ask amiss and such prayers will not be answered. The whole counsel of God shows the importance of prayer but also praying rightly. We do not always know how God will answer prayer but as Christians filled with the Spirit we know when it has been answered and sometimes we realize that the answer may be "no" or "wait." Sometimes the answer comes through other brothers and sisters in Christ, or perhaps God uses someone we do not know. At other times He may answer in a miraculous way and other times His silence on a question is an answer. However He answers we need to keep in mind that prayer is another way by which we can know God's will.

The last way God speaks to us is through the godly counsel of others. Now, please note we said "godly" counsel. The world's counsel is often tainted by its perspective on life. As is mentioned on the copyright page of this book it is wise in light of the rapidity of change in our world and each individual's unique circumstances to seek appropriate financial and legal counsel before making major decisions. We would suggest that counsel, if possible, should come

from a Christian professional. Be careful though, there are many who use the term "Christian" in their business because they go to a church and want the members' business. There are many who profess to know Christ in this world but few who have confessed Him as the one who has died for them. The testimony of others concerning an individual may be able to help you find the right godly individual.

Godly counsel, of course, is scriptural. The Bible says "where no counsel is, the people fall; but in the multitude of counselors there is safety" (Proverbs 11:14, KJV). The key here is again in the type of counsel. The worldly wise may be helpful and very knowledgeable in the financial maze of rules or in the legalese of the day but they have little understanding of the biblical perspective. So, use the world's experts if necessary to understand its requirements but when it comes to knowing what God wants consider godly counsel.

In summary, then, our Christian financial planning and implementation is influenced by the Holy Spirit in three ways. They are by His Word, by prayer, and by godly counsel from others. It is by using these we truly understand God's will for our lives in the area of finance.

Exercises and Research Activities

1. Take a careful look at the Bible and what we discussed in this chapter and see if you can answer the question: why is every Christian not financially rich?

2. We looked at Christ as the Creator and sustainer. Why is this important in the context of financial stewardship?

3. Why do you think that God has us work in order to secure possessions from Him?

4. Find an article or advertisement that emphasizes the individual as a consumer and write a short summary of what it attempts to accomplish and what the Christian reaction or perspective should be.

5. Write a two-page summary about where "love" fits into Christian financial stewardship.

6. Explain how God directs us if we are the ones who are supposed to be doing the planning. Is not our plan guiding us?

7. Research and present an example of accountability, or the lack of it, in relation to finance.

8. Research and present an example of a financial situation where counting the cost was an issue that was either not considered or was ignored. Discuss the ramifications of the decision.

9. Reflect on the following maxim: the more one gives, the more one receives.

10. Prayerfully consider and select someone to help you be accountable for your personal finances.

11. Take some time to research the Scriptures and try to write a short paper on how God interacts with the world and how that is evidenced in financial stewardship.

CHAPTER 2

The Financial Stewardship Planning Process

Learning Objectives

1. Describe how a Christian views the financial planning process.

2. Develop biblical financial goals.

Lord, I commit to planning.

Lord, I realize that according to your Word you have given me a mind to use for your glory, including planning for the future. Please let your Spirit guide me as I commit to setting appropriate goals and plans. I want your will to be done so please direct my steps. Keep me from seeking the world's riches as I plan and help me seek to plan wisely that which you would have me plan for. Thank you for your love and for the resource of life you have given me.

Assets, Liabilities, Income, and Expenses

To understand the Christian perspective on the financial planning process we briefly define here the key components that are used in various financial planning documents. You can consult a personal finance text to learn in more detail the creation and use of these documents.

Defining the Categories

Most financial reports deal with one or more of four key areas that we will define here. These definitions are based on the standard definition used by most financial people and how a dictionary would usually define the term. In the next section we will deal with how our definitions as stewards might be different.

Assets. The Webster's dictionary basically defines an asset as an item of ownership having exchange value. Most texts are very brief and define assets as what you own. Items of ownership include those things that you may still owe money on. These assets can include houses, land, cars, furniture, savings accounts, and the like. We think the dictionary definition is a bit more accurate. The key is that there is an exchange value. Could you sell it and, if so, what is the fair market value? The fair market value is the price that you could expect to get for the item from a buyer, on the open market in a reasonable period of time, assuming that you and the buyer are free and willing to enter into the transaction or not. As soon as you or the buyer are under some compulsion to buy or sell the price will likely change to the advantage of one or the other and thus the "fair" value is not what would be realized by a sale. It may be more or less. What is important here is that an asset must be fairly valued based on the current circumstances. If you must sell that asset in two weeks its value may be substantially different than if you were going to hold it for an indeterminable amount of time. Also, you cannot value an asset based on its expected future value since the future is unknown. An asset is valued at a point in time so you can determine your financial status at that point in time.

Assets, at times, are further divided into categories. The term "liquid assets" is often used to identify those assets that can easily be obtained in the form of cash. Sometimes called monetary assets, these include savings accounts, checking accounts, certificates of deposit, and cash on hand. A second category of assets often noted is "tangible assets." It is not as if cash is not tangible but these items are considered non-cash items that would need to be sold to get the cash equivalent or make them liquid. These include houses, cars, furniture, antiques, and the like. The value of these items may go up or down over time depending on the asset and the market conditions. This is why they are valued at a point in time. Another category that is sometimes listed separately is "investment assets." These include stocks, bonds, real estate, and other investment vehicles that may incorporate these, such as individual retirement accounts. These would also need to be sold in order to make them liquid at their current market value, thus, they are also valued at a point in time. Their value can go up or down over time although historically these have experienced an increase in value over time.

In summary, then, assets are things that you own that have some value in exchange for them. They are often divided into one of three categories including, liquid or cash assets, tangible assets, and investment assets. Assets are valued at a point in time so that we can create valid current financial plans and reports. We will learn about how these can be used in a plan later in the chapter.

Liabilities. The basic definition offered by a dictionary would be monies owed, debts, or obligations. Another definition the dictionary gives is "something disadvantageous." This definition, although not actually used in this context by most, in a sense is quite appropriate. These are the items that would be opposite your assets in a financial report. The value of these items is usually predetermined based on an instrument, such as a loan, that you signed to acquire an asset. Whereas assets can change based on various market conditions, liabilities often do not. There are a few cases such as variable rate instruments that can change a liability based on market conditions. Liabilities usually change in value as you repay the obligation. So, liabilities tend to go down in value over time usually based on a predetermined schedule of payments. There are certain situations where even with payments the value of a liability goes up. For instance, when you pay less interest than you owe for a particular period, the value of the liability will increase because the interest not paid is added to the outstanding balance. This is sometimes called negative amortization.

"The term "liquid assets" is often used to identify those assets that can easily be obtained in the form of cash."

As with assets, liabilities can be, although not always, grouped into categories. The two most popular categorizations are short term liabilities and long term liabilities. Although these categories are not hard and fast, short term liabilities usually include obligations that are a year or less. These may include utility bills, college fees, insurance, rent, and credit card balances. Long term liabilities often include mortgages, car loans, education loans, and other long term purchase loans. By this list you can see why liabilities might be considered a disadvantage. We discuss this in more detail in the next section concerning the steward's view of these things.

Income. From a dictionary perspective income is the return that comes in as a result of your labor, business, investments, and the like. Basically they are cash inflows into the home and could include other items such as gifts, rebates, and refunds. Most individuals who run into financial difficulties try to resolve the problem by increasing inflows rather than decreasing outflows, this is often an error.

Expenses. Expenses are simply costs or charges. These can be incurred as a result of purchasing, or considered reimbursements for previous funds borrowed. These are basically cash outflows from the home.

We only introduce income and expenses for the sake of the upcoming discussion in the next section on the steward's view of these things but we will certainly get into more detail on expenses later. An important point that is often missed by young people is the relationship between these four categories of assets, liabilities, income, and expenses. Intuitively we know it is good to have assets and not so great to have liabilities, but do we fully understand how to integrate the four categories to maximize our assets and limit our liabilities? Let's continue on and see.

The World's versus the Steward's Perspective

As we have noted earlier, the Bible calls us to be stewards rather than consumers. This can be difficult since the world is constantly bombarding us with the message of consumption. The difficulty is that the more we consume the less we will have to show for the return for our efforts in the "the account."

Exhibit 2-1 shows the four categories in a financial planning view. You notice first of all there is nothing in any of the four categories.

Income	Expense
Assets	Liabilities

Exhibit 2-1. The Financial Planning View - The Categories Empty – Starting from Scratch

That is, we will start from scratch. Let's say our parents have just given us the "left foot of fellowship" from the home. Where do we start in the figure? The question, then, is where are you financially? Let's update the figure

to show a $1,500 savings account and $38 in cash as the only assets we have and no liabilities.

So, in Exhibit 2-2 we have added the savings account and cash. How do the other categories get filled? Now, after hearing our parents' ultimatum, we decide we need a nice cold Coca-Cola while we ponder our future. How will this expense be funded?

Income	Expense
Assets Savings - $1,500 Cash - $38	Liabilities

Exhibit 2-2. The Financial Planning View – The Internal State of Things

We could pay for it in one of two ways: through the cash fund or the savings account. But before considering how cash flows within the picture how do things get into the financial picture in the first place? Where did the cash and savings come from? Where do the liabilities come from? They obviously come from the outside. That is, there are external factors that influence the internal state of our plan. We do not necessarily have to use every possible external factor but there are a number we can look at. Let's look at income. How do we get income? For most of us it is or will be from working at our profession. So we need to add that to the income side – working for Carabba's (nice restaurant). Carraba's in turn pays us and we consider that to be income. But on the outside we must note that there is some type of skill, talent, or profession that we are stewards of that makes us capable of satisfying the employer's needs so that we get paid. So updating the previous exhibit we now include our skill set that the Lord has blessed us with and our work income.

Are there other ways of getting income into the picture? How about gifts or interest from our savings account? We have added these to Exhibit 2-3.

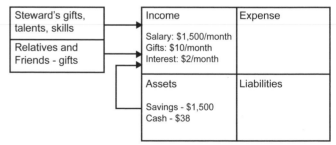

Exhibit 2-3. The Financial Planning View – Income Included

It is interesting to note, now, that an asset can produce income. In fact, as we have seen in the biblical parables we have already discussed, it seems that an asset should return something. Are we using present opportunities to provide for future blessing?

This appears to be one of a number of lessons from the parable of the rich fool in Luke 12:16-21. The rich man's return from the harvest was great but he also misunderstood that asset and its purpose. He saw it as just his asset for making himself merry. He did not recognize God's ownership. As a result, his plan of stewardship, to build bigger barns for himself would have no future blessing in God's eyes. Of course, often missed is the cost related to the tearing down of the old barns and building the new. Was there truly going to be a valuable return on this type of asset after factoring in the costs? Perhaps if, like Joseph, he decided to build barns for the purpose of providing against a famine, then the possible future blessing would be great. So an asset should have a purpose for future blessing and/ or be providing a current return. This is the steward's perspective of an asset.

Assets as the world would see them, as we have noted, are anything of value that can be exchanged for money. As a result, the world by definition includes even items that cost a great deal to maintain and whose function is not truly that of an investment. For instance, the current value of cars is included as an asset on financial statements even though the cost of maintaining and running them annually may outweigh their worth. The same can be said of a house. The world includes the house as an asset but the steward, as with the car, recognizes the home as a substantial liability due to the expenses related to its upkeep.

The problem is not so much where they are listed on the statement but what we think as a result of where they are listed. If we see the home as an investment we think spending more and more for larger and larger homes is a "good investment." The truth is homes are shelters that have substantial expenses related to them, so, although listed with assets, should be viewed as liabilities. Bigger homes just like the bigger barns of the rich fool are not always the way to go. Many people learned the hard way that homes should not be seen as investments when in the late 1980s, and the last few years, the real estate market took a substantial correction and many lost their homes. They did not lose an investment they lost their shelter; their place to live. Exhibits 2-4 and 2-5 now show updated financial pictures from the world's and steward's perspectives respectively.

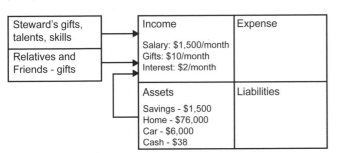

Exhibit 2-4. The Financial Planning View – The World's View

The steward's view sees anything that generates significant expenses as a liability since it does not create a return to the income box that can then be used to increase assets. Cars and homes do not return anything unless sold. Selling them is not usually a viable option unless you buy another, live on the street, or find a place where someone else foots the bill.

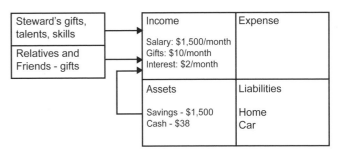

Exhibit 2-5. The Financial Planning View – The Steward's View

Money also flows into our picture from the outside through credit or borrowing. These become liabilities since they generate expenses that must be paid as well as the repayment of the amounts that are owed. The strange thing about borrowing is that it comes in through the liability quadrant and is really never seen as income. Where do the funds go generated by the borrowing? They either exit through the expense quadrant to be seen no more, or generate another asset. Of course, depending on the asset (like a home or car), the steward might view the purchased asset as another liability. What we find as a result of all this is that money only flows out through the expense quadrant. So now we can update our two financial pictures appropriately to reflect this in Exhibits 2-6 and 2-7.

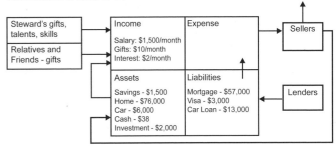

Exhibit 2-6. The Financial Planning View – The World's View Complete

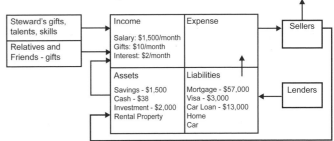

Exhibit 2-7. The Financial Planning View – The Steward's View Complete

Developing a model like this is very important so that we can understand where the money we generate goes. The world encourages us to increase the size of the expense box. When that happens, and times get tight, the world then says to increase the income box and if that is not possible then increase the liability box. Rarely does the world look at increasing the asset box or reducing the expense and liability boxes. The steward recognizes the need to increase the asset quadrant by reducing the expense and liability quadrants. As good stewards, we really want our model to look like Exhibit 2-8.

Exhibit 2-8. The Financial Planning View – As the Steward Really Views It

This exhibit shows several important points that we need to keep in mind as we move forward into planning. First, the steward's liabilities are few and relate not to having debt but maintaining the resources. There are no loans on the home or car but there are still taxes, utilities, maintenance, and insurance among other things to be paid. By having few liabilities the steward is able to focus income on the asset area where much return can be developed. The world says to use other people's money to leverage purchases including assets but the Bible says that the lender rules over the borrower. (Proverbs 22:7). Second, the steward keeps the expense quadrant smaller than income in order to use income to develop assets. The world says to increase expenses to look better but the steward wants a good return and is not misled by vanity and short term gains. By having a smaller expense quadrant the steward has the ability to purchase assets without using excessive liability. Third, the assets quadrant proportion-wise continues to grow for the steward. Lastly, if the assets continue to grow then the income from those assets continues to grow and the need for outside income is reduced allowing more time to devote to the Lord's work and the steward's ministry. By the way, we did not forget about that nice cold Coca-Cola but now we think you understand enough about the model that you can decide where the money will come from.

As a side note, what most people do not realize is that most millionaires in America do not inherit their wealth but rather take the view of the steward above and are careful with their resources. They focus on assets and, though their goal or purpose of being rich may be unbiblical, their wise use of resources makes them successful with the world's mammon. Let us seek to be wise stewards using the resources that we know are a provision from the Lord in a manner that is well-pleasing to Him and we will be blessed and He will be glorified.

Developing a Financial Plan

If you have been using a financial planning text in conjunction with this book then you will likely see a series of steps in relation to financial planning. We will just note a few things here in summary concerning that process and the Christian perspective of these things.

The Financial Planning Process

There are usually five to seven steps in the financial planning process depending on the text being used. It does not pay to skip steps. Remember our discussion under the biblical perspective that we need to seek, think, and do. Each of these also should be considered as a part of this process. Here we will briefly discuss a good first step related to the overall process, and then you can consult any standard personal finance book to see a full treatment of the process.

Financial Analysis: The Current State. Most financial planning models include as the first step a review of the financial state. If it does not, then add it on. It's amazing how many people attend to their financial affairs without really knowing what their current state is or how they are using their current income. Most do not bother to look at the current state of financial matters until they are in very deep trouble. The importance of analyzing our current financial situation cannot be understated. How can you plan your financial goals or other goals, for that matter, unless you know how things currently stack up? Have you ever noticed how Paul was often sending brethren to the local churches in the New Testament? Did you ever notice why? Let's take a look. In Philippians 2:9 Paul says "But I hope in the Lord Jesus to send Timotheus to you shortly, that I also may be refreshed, knowing how you get on" (JND). The KJV actually uses the term "know your state." Paul obviously is concerned as to whether things are going well with the Christians at Philippi. It's not a financial issue although we are sure Paul would be just as interested about that as he was for the financial state of those at Jerusalem.

What is important here is that Paul, by knowing their state can then determine what the next step might be. Based on the findings he could exhort, encourage, teach, and send others to minister, or take a collection. It is clear in Colossians 1:7-8 that Epaphras has given a report on the state of things at Colosse. As a result Paul is writing the letter to the Colossians to deal with some of the needs he is hearing about. Again the important thing here is that we need to know the state of something before we can make plans and act. Proverbs says, "also, that the soul be without knowledge, it is not good; and he that hasteth with his feet sinneth" (19:2, KJV). See the connection between knowledge and planning? The one who does not plan and goes full speed ahead is headed for failure. Before taking steps with the feet analyze your financial situation.

This analysis of the current state should include a net worth statement, a current budget or spending plan, and a current debt analysis. These are all usually covered in detail in standard financial planning books so we will not go into detail here. There are also many examples of worksheets for these reports in standard financial planning books as well as on the Web.

Developing Financial Goals

Assuming you have completed a financial analysis to see your current state, and have learned about planning worksheets on your own (net worth, budget, and debt analysis) you are ready to take a serious look at identifying financial goals, alternatives to reaching those goals, and choosing from among those alternatives. Once you have chosen the road you wish to take you can then update any planning worksheets to reflect your new plan. These new worksheets along with your financial goals will be the documents that form the basis of your financial plan. In the ensuing chapters we look at the biblical perspective with you to understand all the different facets of the financial plans you created so that you can identify appropriate alternatives and make intelligent choices to meet the financial goals that you will now create.

Before moving on to the next chapter, review the notes on establishing financial goals covered in this chapter. Based on your analysis of your current situation and desires for the future, write down a set of financial goals using a worksheet like the one given in Exhibit 2-9. This exhibit gives examples of short and long-term goals related to the financial life cycle covered earlier. These goals relate to purchase management, credit management, risk management, investment management, and estate management. When developing financial goals the acronym B.-S.M.A.R.T (the "B" has been added in front to keep in mind the biblical aspect of our thinking) may be of help in keeping the important characteristics of goal development in mind:

Be Biblical. Goals such as: we want to get rich or have a luxurious house like the Jones', or do nothing when we retire are goals that should be foreign to the Christian, as far as physical riches go.

Be Specific. Goals should be recorded and be quite specific so that you will know that you have met them. If you have a goal of being a philanthropist that may well be a worthy goal but what does that mean? You would need to be more specific about what you mean by being

a philanthropist. You might mean "creating a foundation that will distribute at least $100 million a year within 3 years" or you could mean that you "will give 15% of your income annually to charity within 3 years."

Be Measureable. Goals should be measurable. How else will you be able to count the cost and evaluate whether you can reach or have reached the goal? Saying we have a goal of saving a lot on our expenses may never be met if we do not define what "a lot" is. Perhaps it would be better to say we will save $200.00 a month on our expenses within 3 months. Also, it might be helpful to break larger goals into smaller ones to make them easier to measure, take action on, and achieve.

Be Actionable. This simply means that you will write the goal in the form of an action. This makes it more specific and identifies the action you will take in order to accomplish it. For instance, when we discussed the goal of being a Philanthropist we used the words "create" or "give." This means your goals will have verbs in them.

Be Realistic. Setting goals that cannot be realistically met are likely to lead to financial plan failure. We want to be the owner of the Boston Red Sox is just not a realistic business goal for us, as much as we may enjoy rooting for the team. There would be business availability, time, and money issues that would make such a goal unrealistic. It does not mean we cannot establish a goal that might seem difficult, but prayerfully consider each goal and then as God leads add it or leave it off the list.

Be Time-bound. Notice how we put time frames on the sample goals we have given so far. Putting a time frame on the goal will help you determine when to begin implementing steps to get there and whether you will be able to in light of other goal priorities. This will also help if one goal is reliant on another being achieved first. Do not underestimate the importance of putting a time limit or an end date on a goal. Having identified time boundaries on your goals will also help you to prioritize your goals which we touch on below.

In the process of looking at the acronym for developing goals (B.-S.M.A.R.T) we actually mentioned a few other characteristics of goal development that the individual should keep in mind and that we touch on individually here:

Be sure to keep written records. All financial goals (as well as other life goals) should be written down as a way of reminding you of what they are. Research shows that those who write goals down are much more likely to accomplish them. Goals can be posted and easily carried with you so that you'll have something to use as a reference as you pray for God's will in these areas.

Be sure to prioritize goals and actions. You will likely have many financial goals and it is not surprising that at times they conflict. The issue could be insufficient funds or other resources such as time. Sometimes you will have two very important goals that cannot be satisfied at the same time. This is where prayer and godly counsel can help. In the end, though, you will likely need to make some difficult choices. Be sure to set a priority on your goals in order to keep track of what your current objectives are. If you try to work on too many goals at once you may get frustrated and ignore the plan that you very much need.

Those who would undertake developing financial goals themselves need to have two key attributes; contentment and willingness to do something. These are characteristics of the individual not the goals themselves.

Do not make financial goals out of being discontent with what you have. Making them because you are discontent with the debt you have is a different story. But it is important to keep a biblical balance. We should plan but also be content. Paul says in Philippians 4:11 "not that I speak as regards privation, for as to me I have learnt in those circumstances in which I am, to be satisfied in myself" (JND). Paul found contentment in whatever state the Lord put him in. Does this mean we should not plan? Of course not. James takes the right perspective when he states, "Go to now, ye who say, to-day or to-morrow we will go into such a city and spend a year there, and traffic and make gain, ye who do not know what will be on the morrow, (for what is your life? It is even a vapour, appearing for a little while, and then disappearing,) instead of your saying, if the Lord should so will and we should live, we will also do this or that" (4:13-15, JND). To plan without God in the picture will lead to failure for the Christian. So there is a balance of seeking the Lord, being content, and planning.

Although you may not yet know what steps you want to take to achieve a goal, after you have brainstormed scenarios and chosen alternatives you will want to return and fill in that remaining portion of the goal. That is, what steps are you going to take to make the goal a reality? Remember "doing" is a key aspect of how God uses us. We are not very useful servants of the Lord if we are unwilling to take action. We touched on this under the "actionable" characteristic of goal development. Another aspect of this is that sometimes as you look at your alternatives there are none that are very palatable. The question is, will you, in the will of the Lord, do what it takes? It may mean selling the car or the home, or canceling the cable or satellite TV. If that is what God is showing you must be done to achieve the goals you believe are in His will, will you do it?

Financial Goals Worksheet

Date Set	Goal	Priority	Target Date	Cost	Biblical	Specific	Realistic	Measured
Near-Term Goals								
3/1/2005	Pay off credit cards	High	3/1/2006	12500	Yes	Yes	Yes	Yes
1/1/2005	Save $500 for Christmas gifts in order to pay cash at Christmas	Low	11/1/2005	500	Yes	Yes	Yes	Yes
4/1/2005	Build an emergency fund of $2000	Med	4/1/2006	2000	Yes	Yes	Yes	Yes
5/1/2005	Buy new sofa for under $300	Low	9/1/2005	300	Yes	Yes	Yes	Yes
Mid-Term Goals								
12/25/2003	Become debt-free	High	2/1/2008	43000	Yes	Yes	Stretch	Yes
1/1/2005	Start a retirement fund with at least $5000	Med	11/1/2009	5000	Yes	Yes	Yes	Yes
Long-Term Goals								
1/1/2005	Purchase a home in the Nashville area	High	1/31/2012	163000	Yes	Yes	Yes	Yes
5/15/2000	Earn a doctorate degree in Digital Media	Med	5/1/2010	37000	Yes	Yes	Stretch	Yes

Exhibit 2-9. Financial Goals Worksheet

Exercises and Research Activities

Some of the exercises assume that in relation to planning, the reader understands the concept of the time value of money and how to calculate present and future values.

1. Your grandmother has given you $9,000 so you can purchase a car. Are you better off spending all of it on a car or should you save some of it?

2. You have decided to save money so you can pay cash for your next car. You have figured out that by cutting back on expenses you can save $97 a month. How much will you have in 6 years when you are ready to buy another car assuming you can save at a 3% rate of interest?

3. You and your wife have decided to save so you can pay cash for your home rather than take a mortgage. Together with careful spending you both have committed to saving $440 a month. You plan on buying in 8 years. How much will you have assuming a 6% rate of return?

4. Your uncle has given you a choice of taking $7,000 now or $10,000 in ten years when you will need the funds to help fund your child's education. You expect that you could earn 5% compounded monthly if you were to take the cash now. Should you take it now or wait? Explain your answer.

5. Find some one who owns a home (yourself, your parents, or another) and research how much it currently costs to make it available for living. Include repairs, utilities, taxes, and interest on the mortgage. Consider how much that cost would be for a 10 year period. Compare that cost plus the original price of the home to the current value of the home. What did you find? What would you suggest the rate of return on this investment was? Would you consider it a good investment? Would the rate of return increase or decrease over time?

6. Create a set of financial planning documents for yourself. Include a net worth statement, a spending plan, a debt assessment worksheet, and a financial goals worksheet.

7. If you have a $200,300 mortgage on a home worth $245,215, $4,000 on credits cards, $4,395 loan on a car worth $3,650, $3,000 in savings, $315 in cash, and $900 in an IRA, what is your net worth?

8. Develop in detail a set of financial goals for the next 20 years. Include some thoughts on how you expect to accomplish those goals.

CHAPTER 3

Family Financial Matters

Learning Objectives

1. Identify and describe the role children play in financial planning and how they also can influence another's financial planning.

2. Explain how men and women are different when it comes to financial thinking and decisions.

3. Analyze the ramifications to the family and the financial condition of the family of having both spouses employed.

4. Discuss the advantages and disadvantages of allowances for both children and adults.

Lord, I commit myself to the family unit.

Lord, help me to be careful to consider my family as I make financial decisions. Help me to train up any children you may have given me or may give me in the future to be faithful financial stewards according to your Word. Give me insight by your Spirit to deal with issues that will arise in the family that our actions as a family may result in glory being brought to your name.

The Role of Children

Children play a key role in our financial planning in several ways. Most authors in financial books will note little about children and when they do it is usually concerning how expensive they are to raise. That is certainly one area to look at but there are also the issues of how children influence our financial practices and teaching our children about financial planning. Even if you are young and currently do not have children or do not plan on having children you may find this section interesting, especially if you are one who enjoys helping others who have children.

The Blessing of Children

I believe it is important first to realize that children are a blessing from the Lord (Psalms 127:3). If our initial view is to see them as an expense or some inanimate object that uses our financial resources we will lose out on the blessing that we can receive in loving and caring for what God has blessed us with. Then there are those who have children for the financial gain it brings from the various government programs and the additional tax deductions they bring. In the world there is a spectrum from seeing children as an expense to be managed, to seeing them as a means to financial gain. As a Christian our thinking is not on the world's spectrum. We recognize that children are a blessing from God that must be trained in the nurture and admonition of the Lord (Psalms 127:8; Ephesians 6:4). The Christian also recognizes that just like adults, children must be provided for and resources will need to be carefully considered in providing adequately for any child's growth. Interestingly, then, the Christian should see the child as something he needs to be a good steward of as well. That is, what fruit will abound to the Lord from the child that you are raising? It is not what we spend on the child that will make a difference in the fruit but how that child is raised. It is not how much we invest in the child; it is how we invest in the child that will make the difference.

The Cost of Raising Children

Although as Christians we do not view a child as an expense we recognize that they do require care and feeding. Of course, to provide this requires expending some resources. It is hoped of course that by expending those resources there will be a return on that investment in the child. Certainly we need to keep in mind that if we desire to have children that we are agreeing to make a commitment of resources to invest in that child to help him to grow. Investments in food, clothing, and health care are examples of this. You might be surprised to learn that there are many calculators on the Web for determining the cost of raising a child. You can go to www.bankrate.com or www.babycenter.com to check out a couple of the many that are available. Many articles have been written on the topic and usually there is an

update done by some organization each year. Usually the costs produced exceed $250,000 before college education.

Like all things financial we need to carefully consider what the basis of these calculations are to see if they are realistic. Usually they will take some average for a particular expense area and divide it by the number of children or individuals in the family. If we take housing, as an example, many will divide up the cost of rent (or taxes and interest on a home) to come up with a child's housing cost. To the author this makes little sense unless having a child requires you to spend money to modify your current home to accommodate the child or to move to a larger home. In many cases having a child does not incur any additional housing costs. When we had our son there was no change in our housing costs by adding the child since we had another bedroom in the home. If you have a second child and they can share a bedroom then the same thing is true. Keep in mind that the idea that every child must have his or her own room is relatively new and can lead to much greater expenses by forcing you to buy a larger home. There are benefits in children learning to share a room. Today, too many couples overspend to provide a separate room for each child.

Another category of cost will be food. There will be some incremental cost for each child added to the family. That cost will likely grow as the child ages and eats more. Also, keep in mind as you add children, the cost of eating out increases much more dramatically than does your grocery bill.

A third category of expenses that is usually part of the formula is transportation. As with housing, many of these formulas automatically assume it will cost you more because you will need to buy a larger vehicle. Again this may not be the case. The idea of families with children needing an SUV or a mini-van is also relatively new. A sedan or small wagon is usually sufficient for small families of four individuals or less. If you do buy another vehicle (used or new) because of the addition of a child then your costs may well increase substantially. The additional car payments, if any, the increased consumption of gas for a larger vehicle, and the increased taxes for a newer vehicle in some states, will all apply. The biggest cost may end up being the additional driving that results from having a child, especially as the child grows. This may include doctor visits, school activities, and other outings or sports.

Clothing is another category often included in child cost calculations. If you decide to clothe your children with only new clothing or the name brands, be ready to spend a great deal (although unnecessarily). In reality families really do not need to break the bank on clothing. There are loads of great used clothing available regularly at yard sales, auctions, or at great discounts at clearance sales. You should never pay retail for clothing and never buy an expensive brand name because the other children's parents are doing it. Often you can get great clothing for free from members of your church. It is amazing how much is spent on clothing and this is why these cost formulas appear so large and overstated.

A fifth area that will certainly play a role is the area of healthcare costs. Especially in the first few years, well baby care, immunizations, and various illnesses will likely increase your costs in this area. Healthcare expenses have climbed, and it appears will continue to climb rapidly. It is likely that the premiums that you pay for your health insurance will climb if it is your first child. After the first child there usually is no increase since you will already be on the family plan of your insurer.

Of course, no child cost would be complete without a miscellaneous category. This usually includes items purchased specifically for the child such as toys, books, and bigger things, as they get older. This area of expenses is not mandatory and there is usually room for much savings here.

That gives you a view of the costs that you may encounter as you invest in your children and that the calculators usually include. There may be additional costs included where both parents work such as childcare. Some calculators will account for this as well. We discuss the issue of whether both parents should work later in this chapter. It is imperative that parents assist children in establishing a fund for their college education while the children are very young. By having a fund available students can avoid getting into an unbiblical position of being unable to repay student loans. We look at this issue in more detail in the chapter on making

major purchases. Most financial planning books will give you plenty of detail on taking advantage of tax-advantaged benefits related to education as well. The key is to realize that children can indeed increase expenses but they are better seen as an investment in something that grows (your child) and should produce value and blessing down the road. Also, it is important to realize that the investment expenses for a child do not need to be outrageous and usually can be significantly under what is produced by the various cost calculators.

The Influence of Children

Another key area for young people to understand is the profound influence children have on our spending habits and priorities. Quite often when we have our first child we are so excited that our emotions take over and we will spend much more than we should so our child "can have the best." We will often buy the best of everything whether or not that might help to care for the child. We also have a tendency to go overboard on toys even as the child grows. We are sure you can tell your own stories of children who have had so many toys there could never be enough time to use them all, and in reality many are only used a few times and then put in a toy box never to be used again. What is sad many of these toys are then sold at yard sales for pennies on the dollar. The key point to bring out here is that we need to "think" before we spend in whatever we do. It is no different when it comes to our children.

There are several ways in which we unconsciously spend more because of the influence of our children in addition to wanting the best for them. First keep in mind that if you bring children to shop with you, you will likely spend more than you intended. Children will see many new things and be asking for something every few minutes. What usually happens is the parent gets tired of the constant requests for things and buys something for the child, even if the child already has two of the item that he never uses. Do not bother to bring children shopping unless they are old enough to understand that you have a spending plan and that they need to help you stay within it on the shopping trip. The shopping trip can be a good training opportunity for children, if ready.

The second area of a child's influence is his or her peers. You will undoubtedly be told by a child that they need Tommy Hilfiger shirts or Air Jordan sneakers (oops, got to be careful, they are athletic shoes) and the like. The key reason they need the overpriced wardrobe or other items is that their friends are wearing them or using them. Horrors!!! You do not want your child looking like a freak so you go out and buy them. Do not be tempted to do this. The child needs to learn not to be conformed to the world's view of what is best. It may even hurt the child not to have the same things his friends may have but the key is helping him to see why. That is, do not just say "no" but explain why and show how the savings in not doing so is a benefit to the family. Show how the tradeoffs work. Too many worry about the child's self esteem when with peers but it is those who learn to stand against the world view as youngsters that will be strong Christians as adults. Do not be one of the many parents who overspend as a result of peer pressure your child is receiving. Most of the items you buy will last for a very short time and then are worth little afterwards.

Another area of indirect influence on you is the advertising today that is directed toward children. The goal of the marketers is to reach the children because they know that if they successfully reach a child they will often reach an adult to buy their product for the child. These marketers are not stupid and have done much research in this area. They know exactly how the individual will react to various stimuli and thus how to present their message. It is important, again, here to help the child learn at a young age the financial tradeoffs that must be made in this life so they can make intelligent choices based on thinking through the options.

The Financial Training of Children

Our discussion on children to this point has emphasized showing children how to think from a financial perspective. Our final topic, then, under this section is to provide insights on how we should train our children in financial stewardship and help them acquire this ability to carefully analyze a financial issue and make appropriate choices. By so doing they will be well prepared to make the right choices when they are living on their own. We will try to touch on the key highlights in this area. You may wish to do further reading in a book that deals specifically with this whole issue. Crown Ministries has many good Christian finance books for young children as well as teens available at www.crown.org.

There are 7 key steps in training up a child to be able to deal with personal financial stewardship.

First, the child needs to commit his or her life to Christ as the foundation. As we have already noted, to understand biblical truths one must have the Spirit of God and this is only available through faith in Jesus Christ. It is important for children to recognize what Christ has done for them at Calvary and what He has saved them from. They need to able to rest in His finished work and allow the Spirit of God to make them a new creation. This will enable them to follow the things of God.

Second, the child must understand that God is the creator and owner of all and that we are stewards of what He has given. If children learn that they are only stewards

of what another owns and to whom they will need to give an account, then they will handle finances much differently. We have discussed this aspect in detail earlier in the book.

Third, the child should be able to understand the difference between being a steward and being a consumer. It is important to help children to understand that the world seeks consumption and as a result they will be influenced and encouraged to do so. As parents you must emphasize what the steward does.

Fourth, you need to be a godly example to your children. Perhaps you have heard the axiom "the nut does not fall far from the tree." The idea is that those you produce will be like you. This is no different in the realm of finances. How you train or bring up your children in finances is likely how they will view it when they are on their own. If you provide a biblical example and involve them as we note here they are likely to follow that example.

Fifth, make financial planning and decisions a family affair. Children will learn a great deal if they participate in the family finances and understand how decisions are made. As long as they can understand that the information is for the family and not for those outside they can learn a great deal by seeing the family spending plan and what is truly involved in running a home and the tradeoffs that must be made. They also get an opportunity to see decision-making in action. Children may also have interesting questions and ideas to contribute.

Sixth, provide income opportunities and be careful with allowances. It is difficult for children to learn financial stewardship if they have no funds for which they are responsible or have no part in the family budgeting process. Families need to find a way to give children this opportunity. Later in the chapter we discuss allowances in more detail.

Seventh, keep the individual child in mind – God has made us all differently. As we already know God has given each individual different capabilities, talents, and spiritual gifts. When training our children we need to keep this in mind. It is not a competition among the children or with others in the world, but whether each has been a faithful steward of what God has entrusted to the individual.

In summary, help children to learn and live the financial guidelines noted in this book and followed by you. As the children grow older you can help them to learn the lessons noted throughout this text. In addition, their involvement in seeing how the family finances work in the form of spending plans, decision making, giving, emergencies, and the like will be great lessons for them. You need to work with your children actively to make financial stewardship a reality. Most parents do little to prepare their children to deal with issues in the financial world.

Men and Women are Different!

Perhaps you have seen or heard about the book *Women are from Venus and Men are from Mars.* This author has not read the book but the title alone indicates to him that the author understands there are differences between men and women. This is another area where the Bible and the world often differ. The world tries to make women and men appear the same or perhaps interchangeable. Despite the world's attempts to make the two genders appear the same or equal in every aspect God has made them different. The physical differences are quite evident and some of the ways men's and women's bodies work are different. The fact that the woman bears the children is a significant difference. We could also go into how the women's role from a biblical perspective is different and how quite often the emotional makeup of the two genders is different. That is, we could write a whole book on how we have learned from God and experience that men and women are different. We will not try to undertake that dialogue here but want to recognize that these differences also generally have an effect on how women and men view financial matters.

For instance, how often do men purchase something for the kitchen? How often do women purchase tools for the garage? Now some may, but generally this is not the case. Send men and women into a grocery store and see what they come out with. We are sure it will be different even if given the same list of things to buy. We

point this out here because many of you are or will get married and it's best to realize now that you and your spouse will have differing views on just about all aspects of finance. You will need to discuss this issue candidly with one another.

Even the emotional makeup and how individuals deal with problems are different and can affect the financial plan. Let's say you get into a major argument with the one you love. How does that affect the finances? Interestingly, it does. It has been found that often people will try to get a release from the stress by shopping. What is interesting is that women will do it more frequently at the malls buying clothes and the like but men will go out and buy major things such as cars and boats to assuage the hurt. Neither is good but men really bust the spending plan when not in the right frame of mind.

The key point here to keep in mind as you enter into the marriage relationship is that how men and women view financial matters can be significantly different just because of their makeup. In addition, the environments that each person grew up in can have a significant impact on how they view financial matters. Be sure to keep these differences in mind and discuss the issue up front and learn to work together on the differences.

One final note, the advertisers realize there is still a difference and so often they will market to the sexes differently even for the same product (such as a car). It's good to keep this in mind as well. A great deal of money goes into researching consumer behavior and they know what buttons to push to get you to buy something even though you may not really need it.

Family Economics

How Many Incomes?

Invariably when giving personal financial seminars or courses the question is raised as to what the Bible says about both a husband and wife working outside the home. The idea of a two income home today is quite common in America. This phenomenon, though, is a rather recent one and certainly is not the primary perspective that the Bible teaches. The Bible as a whole emphasizes the man's role as the head of the home (1 Corinthians 11:2, 1 Timothy 3:4-5, Ephesians 5:21-24) and the woman's role in being a helpmate in the home (Genesis 2:18, Proverbs 31:10-31). Keep in mind we are not saying that a woman cannot work outside the home but are just providing a general perspective on what the Bible teaches concerning those who are married. There may be other opportunities for work or service for those who are young or single outside the home. For the most part today, many will dismiss what the Bible has to say about the unique roles of men and women as cultural and thus not applicable to today. This is quite dangerous because anything that one does not agree with in the

Bible can be dismissed as not relevant on some cultural ground.

Based on the teaching of the Bible it seems appropriate for those who are married (and especially with children) to seriously contemplate whether God would have the wife to take on the helpmate role by nurturing any children and supporting the husband. This support, of course, might include selling wares made in the home or harvested from a garden or field (Proverbs 31:24). So the answer to the question of whether a woman should work outside the home is not one that says a woman cannot earn an income if married. Rather, that the wife's income is derived to support the family in a way that does not take priority over her role as one who takes care of the home. The virtuous woman of Proverbs 31 provides an excellent example of one who supports her husband, provides meals for the household, works with her hands to create clothing for the household and still finds time to support the home with additional income from creating and selling items that are a natural outgrowth of work she already does in supporting the home. Thus, to say a two-earner family is unbiblical would be incorrect. It is clear, though, that the source of the second income should be a by-product of the work already being accomplished to nurture and support the home itself. Today women are encouraged to take on positions that take substantial priority over the support of the home. As a result young children are put in daycare and other members of the home must take on the role that rightfully belongs to the wife. The decay of the American family is a sad testimony to a number of poor choices that many couples have made including seeing marriage as something that is temporary and not understanding the importance of the wife's role in the home.

Another key to your decision-making on whether both spouses should work is counting the cost of doing so. The important areas of cost include:

1. **The extra cost of the second spouse working.** Additional transportation, clothing, meals out, gifts for co-workers, and the like can all add up. Many times, if the second parent plans on working part-time the cost of doing so is more than the income from the job.

2. **The cost to the children.** Careful consideration must be given to the effect on children of any decision. Will they be left in daycare or with a relative? How will discipline work? Is it a Christian environment? Generally children are adversely affected when both parents work.

3. **The cost of keeping up the home.** With both spouses working there will likely be little time to do housework, keep up the yard, and the like. How will all this be handled? If you pay others then that cost will need to be considered in the decision process.

4. **The cost of family time.** Keep in mind that with both spouses working both will likely have to share the load of home-related work and both will likely end up exhausted leaving little time to be together to pray, study the Bible, and have time with one another and any children.

As you can see the decision is not easy and the costs can be great so it must be carefully considered. Quite often it is not worth the cost, though many do not realize it until after they have tried it and failed. Seek the Lord's guidance first and He will show you the way.

Allowances and Spending Money

Allowances are quite often an area of significant discussion because there are differing views on whether and/or how they should be implemented. These differences of opinion usually arise due to both the positive and negative impact allowances can have. First, if you do use an allowance it must be for the purpose of teaching financial stewardship. Giving allowances to children to consume any way they wish is unbiblical stewardship. When a child is young an allowance for purposes of financial training may be appropriate but it should gradually be replaced by the child becoming more self-sufficient in earning income either from work around the home or outside the home. Keep in mind that children should not be paid for chores that they do as part of the family unit where all share in the work (cleaning the home, washing dishes, taking out the trash, etc.). Pay should be given for those items that are not normally considered part of the chores or perhaps that the parents might normally do or have someone else do. For instance, if dad usually mows the lawn or has someone else mow the lawn then once the child is old enough dad could pay the child for mowing the lawn. Also, do not pay children for partially completed work. If they are struggling with a particular task you can use it as a training opportunity and help them learn how to finish it right. The key is to pay only when it is complete. To do otherwise leads children to believe they can get paid for half a job which is not always the case in the business world.

Although we have been speaking about allowances for children here we should note that many also believe in adult spending allowances. Sometimes it is referred to as "spending money" or "play money." Some authors suggest that it can be therapeutic and relieve the stress of keeping track of a spending plan. Of course such a concept is not a biblical one. A steward is concerned about how funds are used and to arbitrarily use some set amount without any regard to how it is used means there is no accounting for it. Also, any expenses with so-called "play money" would escape the four question test we give later concerning whether an expense should be undertaken, thus creating expenses that otherwise we would perhaps not undertake. The whole idea of spending or play money seems ripe for abuse and should be avoided.

Working as a Family

We noted when discussing the training of children above the importance of involving them in the family financial planning process. This is true for all members of the household. Keeping the financial house in order is truly a family affair. The following are suggestions for keeping the entire family involved in the process:

Regularly meet as a family to review the current spending plan and make adjustments as necessary. Be sure each member gives an account in the area that he is given responsibility. This means that as a community each member should have responsibilities. Of course, as community members each also shares in the benefits and rewards.

Work at establishing opportunities for all the members of the family to make a contribution to the family through their work as well as creative thinking to help meet community needs. Keep in mind even if you use allowances as an initial training tool that children should still be contributing to the community in some form without payment.

Keep in mind that there are penalties for not contributing as agreed to the community. Accountability is important for all members of the family. There are no rewards for half-done or poor work.

Keep a family list of household items to be purchased so that all can be involved in keeping their eyes open for savings opportunities.

Learn to give as a family as well by praying for, supporting, and communicating with those in the work of the ministry.

Learn to shop together so that you can hold each other accountable to what is in the budget. You can also make it a challenge to see which member of the family will find the best deal on something that must be purchased. Overall, there are many ways family members can work together to be good stewards of what the Lord has provided the family. The key lesson is that it is not just the one who earns the income or the mom and dad that make all the decisions but it is the family together that will be successful in following God's will regarding financial resources.

Exercises and Research Activities

1. Research and present at least one way women and men are different when it comes to financial issues.

2. Assume you and your spouse are expecting a child this coming year. Do some research on what it will cost to raise that child using at least one online calculator. Write a small critique to show whether you think the result is accurate or not, and why.

3. Your 7-year-old daughter is asking for an allowance. Write a brief essay on what your response might be to her.

4. Research an article for the class or group that identifies a bad use of funds for children. Present how you might correct the problems you found.

5. Consider and be prepared to discuss with your class or group the following statement a parent has just made at your school: It is wrong to buy name-brand clothing for children.

6. Research a family that you would like yours to emulate and make a presentation on your selection discussing why you chose it.

7. Perform some research by going to the grocery store and watching families with children. Write a brief report of your observations.

8. What is God's will for the family regarding financial matters? Defend your position with at least five relevant portions from the Bible.

9. Assume you are married and you and your spouse have both decided to work. Make a list of the additional costs you may have to deal with as a result of the second person working.

PART TWO

Managing and Following the Stewardship Plan

Stewardship and Giving

CHAPTER 4

Learning Objectives

1. Describe the biblical perspective on giving and explain why it plays such an important role in the Christian life.

2. Explain the role of the local church in giving.

3. Analyze an organization to determine if it is one that the Christian should support.

4. Explain the biblical perspective on supporting those who minister and how you might implement that approach.

Lord, I commit to giving.

Lord, I need your help in making the right priorities in my life. There is so much in the world that would attract me to use the resources that you have provided me in the wrong way. Lord, I commit to giving to you out of the love of my heart for what you have done for me in sending your Son to die for me. I also commit to saving some of the resources you provide that I might have a storehouse from which to bless you, my family, and others as you guide by your Spirit. Thank you for your generosity to me in all that you have provided. You are a great and awesome God and there is none that compares to you.

In this chapter we discuss the importance of Christian giving, its biblical basis, its characteristics, and the rewards associated with it. We also look at how we can determine to whom we should give our limited resources that will bring the most glory to God.

The Value and Blessing of Giving

As Christians one of the first things that come to mind as we analyze our situation is how much we give to the Lord's work. Because of its biblical basis few Christians will not at least think about it when contemplating either financial goals or its priority in relation to the rest of the spending plan. The author is often asked if God requires Christians to tithe; or whether gross pay or net pay should be used in determining giving; or is giving only to the church; and a host of other questions. Of course, it is not really all that important what the author thinks but it is very important what God has to say, so in this section we will look extensively at the Bible for our answers on the purpose and methodology of giving.

Biblical Giving – the Christian Perspective

In this section we try to understand what the Bible has to say about giving. The key here will be to open our minds and hearts to what God has to say and not necessarily what we have been taught as a practice. They may end up being the same or they may not but we should follow God's Word.

So, what does the Bible say about giving? Well, a great deal and so we should start with the first time we see an offering made to God. In the Scriptures the first occurrence of a word, phrase, or symbol is usually quite informative. Now, many of you may rush to Genesis 14 where the first occurrence of the word "tithe" occurs, but that is not where giving to God starts in the Bible. It is Genesis 4:3-5. This is the first use of the word offering in the Bible and should give us some insights to what giving is all about. Here we have the story of Abel and Cain's offerings. It is clear from the context that God had revealed to them that when they bring an offering it is to be one that requires the shedding of blood, which is clearly a type of the offering of Jesus Christ. This is why Abel's sacrifice was acceptable and Cain's was not. But what do we learn about giving here? First the offering was brought to God. The giving, if appropriate, resulted in acceptance of the offering by God. Second, and related to this, is that the giver did not give expecting something in return. Third, the gift was a form of worship – a sacrifice sweet-smelling to God and so we learn worship is giving to God. Fourth, the gift is of Christ. The sacrifice of the flock was symbolic of Christ, so when we give we give that which is of Christ. Fifth, it appears to have been voluntary. Although they knew what type of sacrifice was to be given the issue of when they brought it was not developed here. There could have been a particular time

but we are not told here. It certainly was not based on the Law of Moses since that had not arrived yet. Interestingly, two things we do not learn about here are the frequency and the quantity. Yet those are the first things we might think of if someone were to preach to us on the subject.

The first occurrence of the word "offered" in the Bible is in Genesis 8:20-21. This describes the offering Noah made to the Lord after he left the ark. Again there is no mention of frequency or quantity. In fact, we see the same elements as we saw in Genesis 4. This appeared to have been a voluntary offering of thanksgiving to God as an act of worship – a sweet-smelling savor unto God.

Next in Genesis 12:1-8 we see that Abram, after his call by God, built an altar to the Lord. We are not told what he did on the altar but we have a good idea based on the previous two examples.

We now come to Genesis 14:20 where we see the use of the word "tenth." Here again there appears to be no prescription. Abram out of thankfulness gives to the priest of God an offering of the spoils of battle (this is noted specifically in Hebrews 7:4). Here again it appears voluntary, out of love for God and an amount chosen by Abram from the spoils of war. We know the spoils consisted of goods and food (v. 11) and Abram gave a tenth of these spoils to the priest. If we were to use this section alone (which many do) to understand giving, men would only give a tenth of what they earned in warfare. But we see a trend of what giving is about. By the way, this is the only time Abram is reported giving a tenth of anything to God.

There are many mentions of offering in Genesis as in the offering of Isaac in Genesis 22:1-14. There we also see the first occurrence of the word "worship," but the only other mention of tithe is in relation to Jacob in Genesis 28:20-22. It is a vow and so we do not see an actual offering. Although voluntary we would be hard-pressed to use this section for the basis of giving since Jacob was not really giving but making a deal with God. The happenings of Jacob in the following chapters indicate he was not in a place of blessing for quite a while.

When the Mosaic Law came along giving was instituted as a requirement of the law. What did the law require? First there was the Lord's tithe in Leviticus 27:30. This appears to be what is described in Numbers 18:10-11, 17-18, which belonged to the Levites and is sometimes called the Levites tithe. The Levites ministered for God and did not earn a living on the outside so the other tribes gave a tenth of their flocks, grain, and fruit to help support the Levites. In a sense it was like supporting the government of Israel (theocracy).

Deuteronomy 12:10-18 speaks of a second tithe that was instituted on the taking of the Promised Land to be taken to Jerusalem to be eaten together as a family. This is often called the festival tithe. In Deuteronomy 14:28 we have a third tithe offered every three years for the welfare of those in the city such as the fatherless and widows. It is not clear if this was a modification of the second tithe or in addition to it. Other offerings and taxes included: not gleaning the fields (Leviticus 19:9); Nehemiah 10:32-33 speaks of a temple tax; every seventh year all debt was to be forgiven and the land lie fallow (Exodus 23:10-11).

What we basically find when we look at tithing is not a gift to the Lord as a form of worship but a requirement by God as the king to fund the government of Israel. This was the equivalent to our tax system today. But if that is the case where is the giving under the law like we saw in Genesis? Well, it is still there. That is, Israel still gave free-will and firstfruits offerings as gifts to the Lord beyond the required amount to fund the government. We estimate that the Israelites gave 20-25 percent of their production to the Lord to support the nation's government and welfare programs. But there were firstfruits and free-will giving beyond this (Exodus 35:4-10; Numbers 18:12; Leviticus 22:18-23; Deuteronomy 16:10).

Deuteronomy 16:10 says "and thou shalt keep the feast of weeks unto the Lord thy God with a tribute of a free-will offering of thine hand which thou shalt give unto the Lord thy God according as the Lord thy God hath blessed thee." Exodus 35:5 says "take ye from among you an offering unto the Lord; whosoever is of a willing heart, let him bring it, an offering of the Lord: gold, and silver, and brass." Now this is giving. In fact it seems to speak in the same fashion as we saw in Genesis. A voluntary gift in proportion to what God has given. These are noted at a particular time but there are numerous free-will offering passages that show God's desire for man to give voluntarily as he has been prospered. All seem to have the attribute of worship; giving that is a sweet-smelling savor to God.

So, thus far we have learned that tithing and giving are two different things in the Old Testament. Giving relates to free-will offering and tithing to funding the government of the nation of Israel. Israel was supposed to do both, giving up to 25% for funding the theocracy and priesthood, and free-will offerings on top of that out of love for God as an act of worship. The difference between the two thoughts under the law and the plain examples of free-will offering in Genesis make it clear that these are different things.

That brings us to the New Testament. What is the Christian supposed to do as far as giving goes? Not surprisingly giving has not really changed. Before getting into giving in the New Testament let's look at the role of tithing. There is no surprise here either and it is just like the Old Testament. The tithes funded the nation of Israel (including its government and priesthood) and the Lord Jesus himself said that this was proper for the Jew to do. Keep in mind that at the time our Lord was present here in body the Jews also paid the Romans taxes (talk about double taxation!!) In fact, there are only four passages

where the term tithe is used in the New Testament and not surprisingly they all deal with the nation of Israel and not the Christian. We have already noted Hebrews 7 where it speaks of Abram and Melchisedec (1-9), showing Melchisedec as a type of Christ. It is not intended to show anything about tithing and even if it were we have looked at what the intent was there.

Two other occurrences deal with the same situation with our Lord. The Lord tells the scribes and Pharisees they should have done the tithing but not left the weightier matters of the law undone (Matthew 23:23; Luke 11:42). This, again, deals with tithing to support the Jewish nation's government that had not ended yet since Christ came to offer them the kingdom (which they subsequently rejected). As Jews they should have been tithing but were lax in other areas. The only other mention in the New Testament is Luke 18:12 where the self-righteous Pharisee is praying to the Lord how marvelous it is that he tithes all that he has. Obviously this is not teaching that the Christian should tithe but that it was customary for the Jews to do so based on the law.

That is all the New Testament says about tithing (we use the word not to mean a tenth so much any more but the action of giving what you have set aside). Nothing is written to the Christian or the church concerning tithing. That is because tithing is different from giving. Tithing of 25% or so was for the funding of the theocracy. This makes sense since the Christian is not funding the nation of Israel. That is, the church has no government as we know it because Christ is its head and we are all members of that body. Christians live in the world under various forms of human government but not a theocracy. Thus, they pay these forms of government taxes to provide for the nation in which they live. So, what Israel paid then we now end up paying as taxes to fund government programs. Israel is a little different because at times it was a government that was governed by another such as in the Lord's time. The Romans were in power so Israel not only paid for their own government and priesthood but also helped Rome by paying taxes.

The issue is often raised that tithing came before the law so it applies to all. This is not true. The idea of a 'tenth' came before the law but tithing as defined in the law was unique starting with the law. Nonetheless, even if tithing as defined in the law came before the law, it does not necessitate it applying to the Christian. Animal sacrifices came before the law and yet we do not continue to perform them. The Sabbath came before the law and yet we do not observe it although the Lord did. The key is understanding that which applied to Israel quite often does not apply to the Christian or the church. This is why Paul often in the epistles had to keep reminding the saints not to get hung up in the ordinances of old. They had been put aside and Christ had presented a new and living way.

Well then, what is the Christian to do? The same as free-will giving in the Old Testament. Let's look at the New Testament perspective on giving and we will find it is no different than the Old. When tithing is properly understood, then giving as the Bible describes it is consistent. From the gospels, which do not deal with the church or the Christian specifically, and the epistles, which are written to the Christian believers in various churches, we learn the following key things about giving:

Do It Willingly. Mark 12:41-44 is the passage concerning the widow casting her gift into the treasury. This widow did not just give a certain percentage nor was she compelled to give what she gave. In fact, most would have been quite understanding if she did not give because of her financial situation. The issue is not how much she gave (two mites) nor how much of her living (100 percent). The issue was the heart. She gave willingly out of love to the Lord, and as a result, she is blessed to be recorded in the Scriptures as having done so. The same thing applies to Zaccheus when he gave half of his goods to the poor (Luke 19:1-10). That still likely left him a wealthy man yet the Lord did not condemn him for not giving more nor for giving too much. The issue once again was the willing heart. The epistles also show the same idea in 2 Corinthians 8 where Paul speaks on giving. He says "I speak not by commandment" (v. 8). He is not commanding giving. In fact, several times he notes the importance of willingness "…that there was a readiness to will…" (11) and "for if there is a willing mind…" (12). In 2 Corinthians 9 he continues "each according as he purposed in his heart…" (v. 7). We believe we see that giving is to be done willingly just as it was done in the Old Testament. It is not an issue of law or government, but of love.

It Involves Everyone. Paul says "let each of you…" (1 Corinthians 16:2). That does not seem to leave anybody out. No matter how rich or how poor everybody should be a giver to God. Even if you're a student at school God is including you. He wants everyone to experience the opportunity to give out of a loving heart.

Do It Cheerfully. Going back to Zaccheus, did you notice how excited he was? Now, part of that was just having an opportunity to be with Jesus, but look at what it says about Zaccheus when Jesus tells him to come down "…and received him with joy" (Luke 19:6, JND). That joy of coming to know the Lord overflowed in liberality. Paul again in 2 Corinthians 9 says about giving "not grievingly, or of necessity, for God loves a cheerful giver" (v. 7, JND).

Do It From What You Have. God does not expect us to go borrow money for His work. He already owns everything. God has allowed us to be instruments in His work rather than doing it Himself directly. This allows us to show our love to Him. Even the widow who gave the two mites gave from what she had – in her case it was all she had. Paul in 2 Corinthians 8 notes in relation to a man giving "a man is accepted according to what he

may have, not according to what he has not" (v.12). In the previous verse as well it says "…out of what ye have" (v. 11). 1 Corinthians 16:2 says "…as God hath prospered." There is no specified sum but we are told it comes from what we have been given and should be done in liberality (2 Corinthians 8:2).

Do It as a Sacrifice-As Worship. Some people do give in what we might term a sacrificial manner as the woman with the two mites, but this is never a requirement of the giver. When we see sacrificial giving in this way, we see it as it must be difficult to do, to be accepted, or cause a hardship to be true giving. We believe this is not what sacrificial giving is about since to do so is putting a constraint on the giving which negates all of the other Scriptures we have just noted. It is not the amount of the gift or how much of a sacrifice it is, but it is a sacrifice as in worship. All Christian giving should be seen as giving to God in the form of worship. In this sense all giving is sacrificial, if done in the spirit of worship. This was the problem with the Pharisees. It's not that their giving was wrong, but they did it for others to see, it was not a sacrifice of worship to God. This is why Paul exhorts that the laying in store be done on the first day of the week (1 Corinthians 16:2). This is the Lord's Day and the day on which we worship Him. As we saw in the Old Testament when we come to bring a gift to God it is worship. It is no different for us as Christians today. Do not focus so much on yourself (making a gift sacrificial) but on Christ (offering a gift as a sacrifice).

Do It Regularly. We just noted 1 Corinthians 16:2 where Paul notes that we should lay in store on the first day of the week as God hath prospered. It appears that since community worship is done on the first day of the week on a regular basis and giving is part of that worship we are to do it then.

"Let us do good towards all especially towards those of the household of faith." Gal. 6:10

We realize what has been presented here may be a surprise for many who have been taught that we are to tithe or give through various quota systems and fund-raisers. Until we studied the issue for ourselves and saw what the Bible said we followed the same traditions that most others have followed. In reality giving in the Bible is free-will and examples range from very small up to everything a person has. If you find giving ten percent is what the Lord would have you give, that is fine but keep in mind that He may also have you give more based on how He has prospered you.

The Value and Blessings

We should take a moment to understand why giving to God is important. That is, why does the Bible encourage us to give? As with all things in God's plan there is a purpose and this is no different. We learned a great deal about what the Bible has to say about giving in the last section and so we saw glimpses of His purpose in it there. The key reasons for giving are:

As Devotion or Worship. That is, giving is done to demonstrate our love to God as He has done to us. 2 Corinthians 8 says "for ye know the grace of our Lord Jesus Christ, that for your sakes he being rich became poor, in order that ye by his poverty might be enriched" (v. 9, JND). Paul was showing that giving was an expression of the saints' love to God as Christ giving His life was an expression of His love to the saints. We see an example of this type of love given by the woman that anoints Jesus' feet with the ointment and wipes them with her hair (Luke 7:37-38). Hebrews 13:15 notes that we should not neglect doing well and sharing; for with such sacrifices God is pleased. It cannot be any plainer than Philippians 4:18 that states concerning the Philippians' gift to Paul "But I have all things in full supply and abound; I am full, having received of Epaphroditus the things sent from you, an odour of sweet savour, an acceptable sacrifice, agreeable to God" (JND).

To Help Others. 2 Corinthians 8:4 speaks of the gift from the churches in Macedonia to help minister to the saints. 2 Corinthians 9:12-13 notes that the gift from the Corinthians would be for that which is lacking among the saints but also an avenue of thanksgiving to God, which relates back to our first point. In Acts the saints did not view their goods as their own but God's and as there was need they sold something and brought the proceeds to the apostles to minister to those who had need (Acts 4:32-35). Paul makes a general pronouncement that emphasizes that Christians are to help the saints saying "so then, as we have occasion, let us do good towards all and specially towards those of the household of faith" (Galatians 6:10, JND). John also makes clear that helping other believers is important saying "but whoso may have the world's substance, and see his brother having need, and shut up his bowels from him, how abides the love of God in him?" (1 John 3:17, JND).

To Help Those in the Ministry. Another purpose in giving is to support those who minister in the Lord's name. In the New Testament church the teachers and evangelists were supported this way. Elders (sometimes called bishops, pastors, or presbyters) and deacons, of which there is always a plurality in the local church, helped to keep order in the church and watch over the saints and feed them from the Word as well. The elders focused on the spiritual aspects of the ministry and the deacons on the temporal ministry. Although there is nothing noted about financial support for deacons in the Bible some of the same concepts we note here may well apply to them. Paul emphasizes, though, the support of those in the spiritual aspect of the work. The teacher clearly is to be ministered to as we see in Galatians 6:6 that states, "let him that is taught in the word communicate to him that teaches all good things" (JND). Support for the evangelist is appropriate as is noted in 1 Corinthians 9:14. In 1 Corinthians 9:9-11 Paul, in using a quotation from Deuteronomy 25:14, is noting the importance of his legitimate claim to support from the source of those who received his ministry. Verse 11 says "if we have sown to you spiritual things is it a great thing if we shall reap your carnal things?" (JND). The same truth seems to apply to elders in 1 Timothy 5:18 which quotes from the same verse in Deuteronomy 25:14. Paul says "let the elders who take the lead among the saints well be esteemed worthy of double honour, specially those labouring in word and teaching…" (JND).

For Spiritual Blessing. God emphasized to Israel that if they were obedient and gave as directed they would be blessed. Jesus confirms this same thing to the Jew. But the key was their attitude of heart. This is why the Pharisees, though they may have given generously, were not blessed. Their purpose in giving was to be blessed, not by God but by men. 1 Corinthians 13:3 states "and if I shall dole out all my goods in food…but have not love, I profit nothing" (JND).

The Bible does note that as Christians we need to sow bountifully that we might reap bountifully (2 Corinthians 9:6). Luke 6:38 also seems to envision this same thing where it states "give and it will be given to you." Now we see that Luke 6 really relates to the kingdom Christ was offering to the Jew but there are lessons for us as well. But we are hard-pressed to see the physical nature of the things applied to Israel as relating to the believer. Paul is always emphasizing the spiritual blessing and reward for the believer in Christ in this age after the kingdom was rejected by Israel. Where were Christ's blessings in giving his life? They are in the heavenlies. He is our example. He gave all that there might be a great spiritual harvest of blessing. We have already seen that giving with the desire to get rich via a return is not God's plan unless the believer desires to be rich in spiritual blessings in Christ. Paul makes this clear in Philippians 4:17 where the saints' giving was not because Paul desired a gift but he desired to see their giving so it may abound to their account. Verse 18 then emphasizes the spiritual aspect of the gift. Then verse 19 emphasizes that God shall supply all their needs. Not only does the Christian have rich blessing in heaven, but God will take care of his needs (not necessarily desires, or giving riches) on earth. Perhaps it is best said that we are to set our affections on things above which means when we give, we give that He might be glorified and then we are blessed in knowing that God is satisfied with the gift.

The Role of the Church

We have already noted a number of verses that relate to giving and the church and so we will summarize here how your giving relates to the local church so you can be sure that you are being a good steward of what God has entrusted to you. We learn the following key points concerning giving and the church:

Church is a Storehouse. The church is the conduit for Christian giving to saints in need and to the ministry in general. Paul notes in 1 Corinthians 16:2 that we are to lay up in store each week. Some will suggest this could be at home, others within the local church, but in either case the context shows that the church together is giving the gift.

Funded by Believers. There is no indication that the local church and the ministry are ever funded by the unbeliever, as we often see today with fund-raisers and the like. Paul says in the same verse "let every one of you." He is speaking to the believers. Thus, as a believer it is important that you give.

Helps the Saints and the Ministers. We have already looked at the details of the purpose of giving so we will not cover them again here. It is clear that the local believers support the needy such as widows indeed (1 Timothy 5:16) and the ministers of the word (1 Timothy 5:17).

The Focus is People. Most, if not all, of the funds spoken of as gifts in the New Testament were focused on helping people in need or working in the ministry. A large portion of the funds you give to a local church should be for that purpose. Often today we see huge sums being spent on construction and upkeep of buildings that are perhaps used several times a week. We know of churches today that still meet inexpensively in a home or hotel so that more funds can be given to those ministering or in need as Paul shows in Scripture.

Determining to Whom We Give

The last section of our discussion on giving is an important one. How do we determine where to give? There are so many "ministries" looking for funding that it seems impossible to determine where the real needs are. If this is how you feel then you are right. The truth is there are many ministries whose purpose is well intentioned but not of the Lord. In addition, there are many non-Christian organizations in the world that do honorable things that seek our support as well. What are we to do?

Well, it would be best to look to the Bible and, interestingly, everything that we learn about giving in the Bible we have pretty much covered earlier. That itself should tell us something. In reality our giving can be very focused and if the local church through its deacons are good stewards and are spiritually mature, the proper needs of the ministry would be met. Based on what we see in the Bible we need to look at the following:

First determine that the local church is following sound stewardship principles as we have discussed in this book. A church's stewardship of its funds is an excellent indication of its spiritual health. If a majority of the funds go for buildings, grounds, and staffing (other than support for teachers and elders laboring in the Word) then you may want to investigate a church that is more biblically sound.

Second, once you are serving in a church that is sound, do your giving through that local church. Let the mature deacons and elders of the church who should have mature spiritual minds determine whether a particular ministry should be supported. Since there are a multitude of elders and deacons there is a thorough review of the use of funds and to what needs they are going. They can look beyond the methods of men to see what is spiritually strong and sound.

If you desire to determine these things on your own you will need to review each ministry very carefully looking at 1) its spiritual state, that is, does it follow biblical teaching?; 2) the financial reports to see if it is a good steward of what God has already provided them; 3) its leaders to see if they are setting biblical examples in how they conduct themselves and how they seek funding; and 4) praying and seeking godly counsel from others as you try to ascertain which ministries to support.

Third, anonymously support the needs of teachers, evangelists, and individuals in need by suggesting or designating a gift to them through your local church. If a church does not allow this then find a local church that does. The only reason a church should not be willing to do this is if its analysis has found some spiritual issues that prevent them from doing so.

Evaluating Organizations

We do not have time to go into a full-scale discussion of how to look at a ministry but we provide some general guidelines that should be of help. The only ministries noted in the Bible are the local church, the individual in need, the teacher, the evangelist, and the elder, especially if he is a teacher. That is the extent of the supported ministry in the New Testament. Any individual or ministry should be along these lines. Organizations, whose emphasis is political or social reform, although well intentioned, should not be the recipient of your gifts. There is no biblical basis that we can find for these.

This does not mean the local church itself or you as an individual can not minister to those in need in the world. Doing the ministry in the name of Christ is much to be desired. Be careful of fund-raising letters. Many "ministries" today spend more time raising funds than they minister to those they support. Quite often these are professionally written letters by marketing agents who know how to word it just right to get you to send in a donation. Most have pre-written letters ready to send out for the next donation as soon as they receive the first. They are using the methods of men to try to fund God's work. There seems to be a constant bombardment from Christian ministries saying that without our support they will fail. A ministry occasionally letting the saints know of its needs is fine, but for most it is a daily or weekly call. Is the ministry really of the Lord if it is constantly soliciting funds? It would at least cause us to raise the question. In the New Testament, the servants of the Lord were serving and letting God do the providing.

You may occasionally desire to help an organization in the world. Again we recommend that support to the world be done through the local church. This way God can receive the glory for any help given. Also keep in mind that worldly organizations, though perhaps well intentioned, may not be the kind of stewards you would like of the funds, nor necessarily use them the way you had hoped.

Assuming, then, that to this point you know of a number of ministries that you might be interested in supporting, what are some guidelines in choosing which of the many you should support? Below we list some of the suggested guidelines by MinistryWatch.org with our own synopsis of the meaning of that guideline in carefully reviewing organizations that you may wish to send financial support:

Transparency. Organizations should be open to sharing important information about its ministry including clear financial reports. Evidence that the organization relies on the Lord for its support and not on high-pressure fundraising approaches should be expected.

Truth. What the organization claims it does is what it does and there are no known disputes about its claims or with its proper legal functioning as a non-profit organization with the appropriate government entities.

Values. The organization should not be "Christian" in name only. It should demonstrate a commitment to the Bible alone, ministering in the name of the Lord Jesus Christ, and a desire to bring glory to God through His Son. The goal is not is to have a ministry just as a business or a means to enrich the ministers involved in the work.

Sectors. This means checking into what the organization is involved with to determine if it meets the end goals that you desire to support. If you are interested in the evangelism of children it is good to verify that a significant portion of the funding and work go to that area. Some organizations have more than one function so it might be good to understand how these multiple functions are maintained and supported.

Resourcefulness. How careful is the organization in trying to fulfill its mission and how it uses the funds entrusted to it. Elaborate organizational structures, large endowments, and inefficient use of funds would lead us to question whether we should be supporting an organization.

Giving to a Christian organization requires careful review and diligence. Along with the guidelines provided here you can also check other good Web sites for information on organizations and/or wisely choosing an organization for your support. The reader may want to check www. ecfa.org to see if an organization follows sound financial principles or look at www.guidestar.org for additional guidelines on choosing a good organization.

Individuals in the Ministry

As we noted at the beginning of the last section the New Testament emphasizes the local church, and the ministry of individuals. Many organizations do a fine work but there are also many individuals who like Paul, Barnabas, and Timothy serve the Lord entering the work of the ministry in dependence on God to provide through His people without doing any fundraising or support development. Just because there are many large organizations that support many in the ministry we should not forget those who serve in dependence on the Lord.

In addition to those who go out in direct dependence on the Lord are those who may labor in the Word locally, or may be involved in caring for the saints. None of these are ever seen as salaried in the New Testament but this does not mean that we do not have a responsibility to help as the Lord provides.

Early in the New Testament there was a real desire to support those in need and those who ministered without ever having to agree to a contracted salary or having a stipulated monthly amount given to those in need. The difficulty today is that many have lost the zeal of these early brethren in giving as unto the Lord. We now assume that the fundraisers or missionary organizations will take care of what the individuals in the church did.

We should note as well that it is not just financial support for individuals in the ministry. How about providing a meal or a place to stay for a few days? Do you have some extra clothing a Bible teacher could use? How about providing some time to help in an area of the ministry? There are many ways to give the work of the Lord beyond money. Though money can be quite helpful let us not neglect other ways of help.

Now that we have encouraged you to consider those in the ministry, be sure that you prayerfully consider how you might assist just as you would do with an organization. For individuals it might be helpful to seek out references or letters of introduction from another familiar with the ministry work the individual is involved in. Most who go on into the ministry relying on the Lord are not trying to enrich themselves. If the motivation were to enrich themselves they would likely seek a different path to reach their fleshly desires as some have done by creating a business out of ministry and drawing a salary.

In summary, then, give carefully and for the most part do it through a biblically sound local church that supports the ministry of individual teachers and evangelists, as well as Christian organizations. If you decide to give directly to an organization or individual in the work then consider some of the guidelines suggested and do some research as a good steward.

Exercises and Research Activities

1. Consider the biblical account of the widow that gave all that she had. Why did she give more than a tenth of what she had? In what ways would you follow her as an example?

2. What are the key characteristics that God looks for in one who is giving to Him and His work?

3. An organization that claims to be ministering in the name of the Lord has asked for a contribution. What steps would you take in determining if this is what God would have you to do?

4. In what ways does worship model the act of giving to the Lord?

CHAPTER 5

Managing Inflows and Outflows

Learning Objectives

1. Identify the questions Christians should ask when contemplating a purchase.

2. Describe ways of reducing expenses as a good steward.

3. Determine the true cost of an expenditure.

Lord, I commit to spending wisely.

Lord, thank you for the resources you have bestowed on me. I appreciate all that you have done for me and now commit to using those resources wisely. Help me to be a wise steward of my financial resources and to view expenditures from your perspective. Let me by your Spirit make each purchase as if Jesus were physically with me when making the decision. Guide me and encourage me in the right path that the result of my stewardship might receive a "well done" from you. I look forward to that day when I will be forever with you and the Lord Jesus Christ. Until then, I commit to being a diligent steward who needs not be ashamed.

In this chapter we will build on the foundation that has been laid in the previous chapters and develop more fully the reader's capability to identify inflows and outflows in the spending plan and how to increase the inflows while reducing the outflows. Since this area of finding ways of reducing expenses is not as prevalent in financial planning texts we have emphasized it more here. As a steward we need to be careful how we use the resources entrusted to us. This may be at odds to the way it may be presented in other books.

Planning Living Expenses

Now we come to what is likely the most ignored part of the average individual's personal financial planning and that is the area of expenses. Expenses are payments that are made to acquire items or services that are used and do not return income. It's rather interesting to watch how a financial discussion will go when there is not enough money to make ends meet. Invariably, the discussion focuses on how a family can generate more income with little or no consideration of how to create additional available income by decreasing expenses. Scenarios to make ends meet usually involve borrowing money, having a spouse work, or securing another part-time job. We hope in this section to encourage you to take a very careful look at the expense side of the ledger, especially while you are young, so that you can see the difference that careful expense planning can have on your life and that of others.

What is Really Needed?

As you look at planning for expenses the first question that you should ask when looking at each expense item is "is it really needed?" Now be careful here. We need to distinguish among needs, wants, and desires. Needs deal with our sustenance and are the minimum costs required to live which includes expenses related to generating income to cover those minimum costs. Wants go beyond the needs and speak of a minimum satisfaction level or a point where we feel we will be happy. So a need may be to have a place to live whereas a want is to have a "nice" place to live. Desires go beyond wants and speak of the long term and are that which we feel will bring the optimum satisfaction. So if the want is to have a "nice" place to live, a desire is to have a "luxurious" place to live. Another

example is transportation. The need is a basic way that will get us to work. This might be a car, bus, or train or perhaps even walking or bicycling. The want moves this to being a nice car with CD player and air conditioning. The desire moves it to a sports car with sunroof, surround sound system, and 500 horsepower under the hood.

Do you see the difference? Needs are immediate issues generally not of the flesh (spiritually speaking) and deal with conditions that actually exist. Wants from a biblical perspective can have the idea of need, that is, to be in want or lacking. From an English perspective it leans more toward desire. Wants are short term basic desires that usually will more than fulfill a need and occasionally do not fulfill any existing condition or need. They are of the flesh and thus sometimes are called felt needs rather than actual needs. Desires deal with the flesh as well but speak of a longing for that which one does not have and generally, a need fulfilled is incidental to the object itself. Of course, there are good desires such as the longing our Lord had to share the Passover supper with his disciples (Luke 22:15).

With these thoughts in mind the question becomes where should we focus? This is not easy to answer but perhaps the best perspective is to look at your heart in relation to what the Bible has to say about the world's goods. Certainly providing for the basic needs of your family is biblical and providing for support for the household of faith is important. The difficulty comes in our desire to want the best for our family and friends which can be substantially different than what is needed. Is it biblical to get the best? The issue is one of intent and reality. That is, what is the intention in what our decision is and what is the real result of what is determined? There are several questions that can be asked in determining whether an expense makes biblical sense:

1. Is there, at the minimum, a need fulfilled by the purchase?
2. Does the purchase make sense for a good steward? That is, have the tradeoffs been carefully considered (quality, versus quantity, versus cost)?
3. Does the purchase directly or indirectly honor God and His Word or is the focus on self?
4. Would you make the purchase if Jesus were with you when you were making the purchase?

If you can say, "yes" to these four questions you are highly likely to make a sound, biblical, financial decision. For instance one might ask is it biblical to purchase a Porsche? A Porsche certainly at a minimum may fulfill a transportation need if there is one. It is unlikely that it would make good sense for a financial steward and even if it did would it in reality honor God or would it more likely cause ridicule to God's name or cause a stumbling block to others because it is seen as overly extravagant for the Christian? Would the focus not be on you and your nice car – and the fact that "you have made it?"

Keep in mind by asking these types of questions you will likely make decisions that will not be viewed as very popular in the world. It will see you as depriving yourself of the world's luxuries. Its thinking is to "go for the gusto" since you only live once. The Christian perspective is far different. Also, by asking these questions the focus is taken away form the subjective differences among needs, wants, and desires. The issue is not whether it fits one of the three categories but whether it is a sound, biblical, God-honoring choice. In that case it could belong to any of the three categories. Do not be afraid to ask the questions of each of your expenses; you will find it much easier to follow what is right for the steward.

Spending Plan Busters

There are expense items that occur that can quickly doom any financial plan. It is important to be aware of these and be prepared to deal with them. We call these types of expenses "budget busters." They fall into two categories the "big bang" budget busters and the "silent" budget busters.

The big bang budget busters, as their name implies, have a sudden and substantial impact on the spending plan. These fall into at least four key areas:

1. Insurance
2. Taxes
3. Home repairs
4. Auto repairs

The first two items on the list, insurance and taxes, are not unexpected. The difficulty comes in that they are not paid on a regular basis. Sometimes it is as infrequently as once a year. As a result, if they are not planned for, the bill comes in and all of a sudden there is a scramble to try to pay a significant sum sometimes running into the thousands of dollars. For most families today in America this poses a significant problem. To make the required payment families often make quick ill-advised budgetary decisions that destroy what little planning there may have been when it comes to spending.

The second pair of items on the list, home and auto repairs, are usually unexpected and can occur at anytime. The result is no different, of course, than with the insurance and taxes. There is still a large bill to be paid from a spending plan unprepared to handle it, thus having a profound effect on the family spending plan.

To deal with the above scenarios you must prepare in advance for these possibilities. Be sure to set aside funds each month that can act as an emergency fund for when the auto or home need fixing. It is not a question of "if", but "when" something will fail. Things tend toward decay and after many years of use will fail and need repair. In addition, your spending plan should include an amount for normal maintenance of these items so that major repairs will be less frequent. Usually insurance and tax amounts for the year are known in advance. It is best to divide those amounts by 12 and save that amount each month so that you will have the funds needed to pay the bill when it arrives. For instance, if your auto insurance is $900 every six months then you would need to put aside $150 a month in order to pay that bill twice a year (900/6). By taking these steps families and individuals can avoid poor decision-making based on expediency.

The list of silent budget busters is much longer and we need to carefully consider how each causes havoc to our spending plan. We have identified at least ten expense areas that, without you realizing it, will drain your spending plan resources. Let's review each of them here.

Eating Out. We live in a society that is speed oriented and as a result we are taught to eat out frequently at an early age. The difficulty lies in that while you are learning to eat out it is usually others such as your parents paying the bills. When young people get off on their own they are so used to eating out that it becomes difficult to control not doing it. Eating out can consume large portions of your income and you may not even realize it. The average American family eats often outside the home at the rate of over $2,500 a year. It can happen without you even realizing it because you are not spending it all at once. That's why it is important to project costs over time so you get a real feel for the cost involved. For instance if you spend $4.00 a day for lunch five days a week you will have spent $1,040 annually just to have lunch. That may be fine if you understand the tradeoffs but many do not see the scope of the cost of eating out. What if you decided to have dinner out once a week at $20 each? Again you would be looking at another $1,040 annually just to have dinner once a week. How about a coffee and donut each morning for $2.50? That's another $650 a year. These numbers do not take into account the lost interest in not saving the money. Carefully consider when you will eat outside the home and how much you are willing to spend. If you do eat out use coupons, look for early-bird specials, or use discounts available with memberships you might have either at work or with organizations such as the American Automobile Association (AAA).

Entertainment. Akin to eating out is the category of entertainment. This is another big area of spending for the average American. This includes movies, CDs, DVDs, sports, and the like. The 2007 statistics for American families shows that the average family spends about $2,700 a year on entertainment. The Christian must recognize that the world seeks to have the pleasures of life. Society is becoming more entertainment-based. It has sadly even infiltrated the local churches around the country, so much so in fact, that people now select churches based on how they meet individual needs or entertain them. Most of what we spend on entertainment today would not occur if we just asked the four questions concerning expenditures. This does not mean some relaxation aside to refresh is bad but this type of expense is covered later under vacations. In fact the spending given for this category does not include reading materials, cable TV, or vacations. Significantly, then, these numbers just show expenses for pure entertainment.

Cable/Satellite TV. This is an expense that almost all assume is required for a home and some will likely think you have lost your mind if you do not have it. Of course, this is not the case. One of the easiest savings that can be gained in a spending plan is to terminate the cable or satellite TV subscription. You'll be surprised how much more time you will also have for doing other more productive things. The average American home spends almost $50 a month on cable or satellite TV. Do you realize the cost to you over a lifetime just for the sake of being entertained? At $50 a month, and assuming no inflation and not considering the interest that you lose by not saving the funds, during the average adult life of 50 years you will have spent $30,000. That seems like an awful lot of money to account for as a steward and then not to really have a solid purpose for spending it. What is the return? It's something to think about. By the way if you had saved that $50 a month over 50 years even at a small 5% interest you would have a total of $133,433. Is cable TV a good "investment" in light of that number? Again, just something to think about.

Internet Service. Another area that often is missed when considering a spending plan review is the cost of Internet access. Now, Internet access may be appropriate for educational purposes or for work–related efforts. Still, it is important to review the expense. Many individuals overpay for high-speed services that they really do not need at home. The difficulty is that once you get used to the high-speed service it is difficult to switch. Unless you do a great deal of downloading for work at home or have a home business or offer Web services from home you may want to reconsider the expense. Currently various

DSL and cable access mechanisms cost from $45 to $50 a month on average while dial-up access is around $20 a month on average. This is still a significant difference. If you only need access to email or spend a limited amount of time on the Internet each month then your expenses can be even less. Juno offers free email access and some vendors offer low-cost Internet access for $9.95 or less. Some companies offer communication packages of some combination of local calling, long distance, cell, and Internet. Be aware these plans often include many features you do not need and you may end up paying more than you would if you purchased just the services you need.

Another option to consider is to share the Internet access costs with a trusted neighbor. You could also use free access points at local retail outlets such as those at Panera Bread. The local library or a local university may also provide free public access to the Internet.

Phone Service. As with the Internet services, many overpay for what they need. Carefully consider what your communication needs are. Cell phone plans are quite expensive and most will never use all the features or minutes that are provided. In addition, many have termination and other fees. The kids likely do not need a cell phone. If you need one for an occasional call then you might want to consider one of the pay as you go plans offered by most providers now. TracFone has become a very popular option in this area. With these plans you prepay for the minutes and then they are good for anywhere from 90 days to a year. We spend about $100 a year for cell phones that we use mostly when we are traveling. Check your land phone bills and see if there are charges you can eliminate. Some still are paying for phone rentals even though they would have been paid for long ago. Also check your phone bill for unnecessary charges that have been added by the phone company that you may not be aware of.

You can see that many are spending significant amounts on communication. If you figure the cost of cable or satellite TV, Internet access, land phones, cell phones, and all the features and fees that go with them many individuals and families are spending a minimum of $150 a month and a substantial number are paying over $200 a month. Again we are looking at several thousand dollars a year in expenses. Is it worth it? Again, it is just something to think about. As a case in point we have one land phone line, a basic antenna for TV reception, a single high-speed Internet plan with unlimited use, and two pay-as-you-go cell phones with nation-wide access. Total cost including all fees and long distance charges is about $83.00 a month.

Christmas Gifts. Another budget buster is in the area of gift giving, especially Christmas gifts. Because of the good feeling connected with giving to others we will likely overspend if we have not carefully considered what the spending plan will be. In addition, you must save each month so that when the time comes you will have the funds available to purchase the gifts. Easy access to credit cards is a huge hindrance to discipline in gift giving since it is easy to charge it if you do not have the funds. Few people actually total how much they spend on gifts each year and if you did you would be significantly surprised by the total. The current average is approaching $500 per household and almost 10% now spend a $1,000 or more and this is just for Christmas alone. If we were to add in gift giving throughout the year we are likely looking at double what those amounts are. Some suggestions include cutting back and buying smaller gifts, never pay retail, shopping throughout the year rather than waiting to the last minute when decisions are rushed, and making rather than buying gifts. Remember it is the thought and love that count not the amount or size of the gift.

Vacations. Have you looked at the costs of vacations lately? Depending on the size of your family, costs can run into the thousands. Be careful to plan ahead and avoid the expensive money making locations. The cost of a family or even individuals to get into some of the popular theme parks is getting beyond the reach of many but some do it anyway and hope to find a way to pay later. This is not a good idea. Never charge a vacation unless you can pay it off as soon as you return. When considering vacations consider the purpose and consider the four expense questions we set forth. Will this be an opportunity to relax as a family or is this just a high-priced form of entertainment? Again never pay full price, check with your club memberships for discounts, and consider camping or going to a more out of the way place that does not have the crowds or the high prices.

Adult Allowances. We covered this topic under family matters in an earlier chapter, but like the other items in this list it is one that silently consumes funds that really should be carefully tracked and accounted for. As we noted the idea of setting funds aside for just consumption of any kind without accountability is not biblical.

Pets. Another area where income can be quietly consumed is with pets. We have counseled, in the area of finances, folks who have had a half-dozen or more

pets whose total cost when taking into account food, immunizations, grooming, teeth cleaning, and a host of other services runs into hundreds of dollars a month. Pets are wonderful especially for companionship but they should not allow one to become a poor steward of what the Lord has provided. The Bible speaks about providing for those of your household but we do not think He had pets in mind. Now we do enjoy pets and we had the same cat for almost 19 years but we were careful to distinguish what was necessary for his well-being. We provided food, drink, and an annual rabies shot (required by law). Otherwise, we avoided other expenses.

Bank Fees. Another silent consumer of the spending plan is the bank fees. Banks are great at finding ways of getting your income. As we have already noted use a bank or banks that will allow you to avoid as many fees as possible. Some folks will spend $20-$30 a month on fees and the bank acquires the use of their money as well. Be sure to check for ATM fees, overdraft fees, per-check fees, account service fees, account inactivity fees, and the like. Most bank fees can be eliminated with careful planning on your part.

Subscriptions. Many people are surprised to find that subscriptions to newspapers, magazines, newsletters, and other club-related annual expenditures consume a substantial amount of money. The reason that it is a surprise is because they are paid for throughout the year making the individual expenses seem small, but when they are added up their effect is quite large. Review all organization and subscription expenses you really do not need. Many receive subscriptions that they never read. Consider using the library instead of paying for the subscriptions or share the expense with another believer and share the subscription.

This concludes the review of the largest spending plan busters that will be encountered. Through careful planning and the review of each expense through the lens of the four expense questions provided earlier you can "create" more income than you thought possible and perhaps even more than seeking another part-time job. Taking this section seriously can make a world of difference when you give an account.

The Church as a Community

As we continue our look at planning living expenses we come to another asset that is often overlooked in helping to keep expenses to a minimum and that is the community you have in the local church. In society today we often only meet as a church community for fellowship briefly and then most everyone goes his own way. Yet, there is much that local believers can do together that can help to reduce expenses.

Pool Coupons. Cutting out and collecting coupons may be tedious but when used properly can result in significant savings in the expense category. Doing it as a group can be even more beneficial. First, it will encourage fellowship with others in the church. Second, you will likely have more of a variety to choose from. Third, you will have the support of others in helping you to reduce your expenses and perhaps provide some sense of accountability in your shopping. It also makes the whole process less tedious when doing it as a group. We discuss the use of coupons later in the chapter.

Shop Together. Another way of reducing expenses is by church members shopping together. This again not only provides fellowship for the believers but provides additional support and accountability as they shop. You may also be able to buy some larger items together and split the cost that would not only reduce the individual cost but also cut down on food that is discarded because there was too much to be used in the package in a timely manner. Shopping together can be very helpful for single individuals as well for the same reasons and the savings are likely to be greater since larger containers could be purchased and split. Small packages usually are very expensive per unit of product purchased.

Buy in Bulk. Related to shopping together is buying in bulk. The church as a community might be able to work with some stores or manufacturers to purchase some items in bulk at a lower cost and pass the savings on to the local church members. Products such as paper towels, tissues, toilet tissue, canned goods, pet food, and the like could be purchased in bulk at a discount and then the cost split among the families participating. They would just pay for what they needed at the reduced cost per item. Again this can be helpful for singles and families.

Share the Skills. God has provided many individuals in your local church with a variety of talents and skills. These skills should not only be used for earning an income but for helping the other believers in the local area. Why have believers pay retail costs for services that you could provide at no or reduced cost and thus allow more funding to be available for the Lord's work and savings to support families? Help your local church to start a directory of services that are available for church members at no or reduced cost for its members. Also try to find believers in other local churches who would be willing to participate in areas for which your local church lacks the skills. You might even have days set aside once a month to work together on these areas. For instance someone skilled in automobile repair could hold an auto service day at his home or the church for church members. Perhaps others might get together to cook. Others perhaps can come together to clean or garden. The list can go on but as good stewards we need to work together to reduce the expenses incurred by our brothers and sisters so more is available for His work and for family support through savings.

The local church can play a significant role in helping families reduce the flow of funds out for expenses by working together and supporting each other out of love. The result is not only great financial benefits for the families and the church but great unifying benefits such as the extended fellowship that these opportunities provide.

Determining Expense Necessity

Earlier in the chapter we had discussed the issue of whether a purchase fulfils a need. At that time we asked the following four questions to help determine whether an expense is warranted:

1. Is there, at the minimum, a need fulfilled by the purchase?
2. Does the purchase make sense for a good steward? That is, have the tradeoffs been carefully considered (quality, versus quantity, versus cost)?
3. Does the purchase directly or indirectly honor God and His Word or is the focus on self?
4. Would you make the purchase if Jesus were with you?

Those four questions still remain, but we want to note several other questions that are either related or provide additional insight in making a purchase decision. Also note that the fourth question above is phrased slightly differently than you usually hear. That is, we often hear the phrase "What would Jesus do?" but we submit it is far more telling to ask the question "what would you do if Jesus were with you?" It is interesting to note that as Christians He is always with us by the Spirit so our answer should be the same as if He were physically present with us.

What is the Purpose? This relates to the first of the four questions above. What is to be accomplished by the purchase? Does it deal with a real need? Is it just a feeling that you need to fulfill? As we honestly consider this question we must often realize that most "needs" are not needs at all and the purpose is dubious at best.

Is there a Value? This relates to the second of the four questions above. As a steward we are always looking at the value and return of using financial and other resources. So we need to contemplate the value of an outlay. What would be the result of not making the purchase? Would there be any difference? Would there be a reduction in value of current resources? For instance, to purchase a medication to cure a medical problem would meet a need because without it the value of the human resource is reduced and could cause further harm later.

Is it Necessary? This relates to the third of the four questions noted above and as stated before deals with separating the emotional from the reality of the need. This summer may seem very hot and so you may have the immediate need of cooling off. As a result you may say we have the need for a pool!! But is that what is really needed? It is likely that there is not a real need here for a pool. It is just not necessary. There are many other ways one can deal with heat. Interestingly pools quite often are status symbols that receive little use. There are a number of pools, both in-ground and above ground, in our neighborhood and we have rarely seen them being used, if at all.

Is There a Way of Eliminating or Reducing the Expense? Related to this previous point is trying to consider ways of eliminating the expense or at least reducing it by finding alternatives. Perhaps the need expressed is for a "new" car. On further reflection it is not a "new" car that is needed but transportation. So a "used" car would do in this case thus reducing the expense. But you give it further consideration and realize that the transportation is only needed for work, otherwise the car would sit in the driveway. So now it is no longer a "used" car that is needed but some way of getting to work. Perhaps after further reflection you realize that the five mile ride to work could be accomplished with the bike you already own or perhaps there is a colleague who can give you a ride to work. All of a sudden what was a need for a "new" car has been eliminated. Consider carefully what is really needed and consider all of the alternatives.

Study the Cost Over Time. It is imperative, as we have already noted, to look at the cost over time. Part of our consideration in a purchase should be the cost including lost interest from not saving the money. We have already

noted the cable TV example earlier. Even without looking at the interest issue the actual cost should at least cause you to stop to think about it. Going back to the cable TV example, if we pay $50 a month for 50 years we will have spent $30,000. That alone should seem like a fairly significant amount to pay for the little material that comes from it that can be considered edifying for the Christian. If that were not enough when we figure in the interest if we saved the $50 a month the $30,000 lost now becomes almost $135,000. We cannot see how spending that kind of money can be of any value for the Christian in light of the paucity of the return from the cable TV companies. This is just one example. Every expense should be considered in light of its long-term cost.

If after considering these various questions we find an expense warranted then we should undertake an analysis to determine which actual product or service will be purchased. In the next section we briefly discuss some ways to reduce the cost of an item.

Reducing the Cost of an Item

There are many ways of reducing the actual outlay of funds for a particular product or service. In this section we try to touch on some of the key ones but certainly do not exhaust the possibilities.

Coupons. Manufacturers print billions of coupons each year to encourage folks to purchase their products. It is worthwhile to cut and save coupons for future use. They can be especially useful for groceries where some stores will double or sometimes even triple the value of the coupon up to a certain amount. Wal-mart and other large retailers will also accept coupons. You can save hundreds of dollars a year by using coupons when shopping. If you were able to save $300 a year over 30 years at 6% interest you would have almost $24,000. When one sees this kind of number the benefit of using coupons is clear. There are some important points to keep in mind when using coupons:

Organize your coupons otherwise you will lose track of some savings opportunities, or worse, get frustrated and scrap the whole effort as too much work.

Do not use coupons just for the sake of using one. Use them for items that as a good steward you would normally buy. Manufacturers often use coupons to steer consumers to new products or those where there is more profit for the company.

Look for items that you have coupons for that are on sale at a store. The combined savings may make it worth buying as an alternative to another product.

Be careful of expiration dates and restrictions for coupons. Manufacturers are making the coupons more complex by requiring multiple items or different items, some of which you will never use. Going with some members of the church may make this easier since items you would not use another might. Most coupons today have relatively short expirations. This is another effort by the manufacturers to get you to buy more often and on a whim. Be careful. Some have also restricted their coupons so they cannot be doubled or tripled in value by the store.

Be on the look out for store coupons as well. Many grocery and pharmacy stores offer coupons and many are quite good such as "buy 1 get 1 free." If you do not need two, shop with someone and split the cost. Some department stores also print coupons but quite often have a load of restrictions on them so be careful. Some real deals can be found. When we were visiting our son and his wife in Texas we saw an ad for Coca-Cola at 2 for $5.00 which at this time is still a good price for 12-packs of 12 ounce cans. In addition, it was a grand opening with a coupon for $10 off on any purchase. Since there was little else we were interested in we bought 4 cartons of Coke for free.

Save restaurant coupons so that you can save when you eat out. We keep them in the glove compartment of the car so that if we are on the road we can use them to reduce the costs of meals. We rarely spend over $13 for a lunch for two on the road as a result.

You can find many coupons on the Internet as well, although you should be careful of scams. The scams usually involve you purchasing coupons. You should not need to do this. There are some sites dedicated to keeping track of discounts and coupons being offered by stores. Use the keyword "coupons" in a search engine to locate some of these. A good Christian site is www.faithfulprovisions.com.

Shop Around. If you have several grocery and/or pharmacy stores close by then make a list and shop at each buying an item at the lowest cost among them. Take someone else along from the church as well so you can work together and share the costs. For larger items call around to various stores and get prices. You can also check on the Internet for pricing at many of the larger stores.

Coupon Books. There are many coupon guides that are published throughout the country. The Entertainment Guide is one of the best known and offers discounts on hotels, restaurants, recreation, and other services. There are others such as the one for the Nashville, TN area called "CityPass." These books generally cost from $10-$20. Before you buy one be sure to check that it will have coupons for services that you would, as a good steward, normally use. The intent for the vendors is to create new and repeat business. Giving a discount is to try to get you in the door to try it and hopefully you will return next time without a coupon. Of course, your goal would be to find another coupon if you returned.

Shop the Web. There are many search engines available to perform price comparisons for products. You may find something you are looking for cheaper on the Web. Keep in mind the cost of shipping when buying something off the Web and you may still need to pay sales or use tax on what you buy off the Web even though there is currently no tax on Web purchases in general. Sometimes it is cheaper to go to a local store after taking into account shipping especially for larger items. Also be aware that many organizations overcharge on shipping in order to reduce their product price to make it look more attractive. We have seen some shipping costs that are ten times what it would cost to ship the item. Online auctions can also prove fruitful but the same caveats apply and you need to read the terms carefully since a bid is a binding contract to buy. We have seen many people overbid for an item because they were not aware that they could buy it cheaper elsewhere on the Web.

Auctions and Sales. Auctions and garage sales (sometimes called yard sales or tag sales) can be great places to find bargains, if you do not mind buying something that has been used. Occasionally you can also find items that are new. Again, knowledge is important so know what you should pay for an item before making an offer or bid. Also consider the tradeoffs of cost, quality, condition, and future plans. Also, it never hurts to offer less or ask for a discount. The worst case is that the answer will be "no." Our son and his wife needed a dining room table and chairs in order to have a place to eat as well as for other functional uses. Together we investigated a number of possibilities but each had drawbacks. In going to a thrift store the prices were from $70 for a table that needed repair with no chairs to over $300 for a complete used, but functional set. If we went to Wal-Mart a small table with 4 chairs could be had for around $100 but they were not made for long-term constant use in a home and would likely need to be replaced in the future. In going to a retail furniture store you could get nice dining sets that would likely last a lifetime but could run anywhere from $500 into the thousands of dollars. We did see one set at a discount furniture store that seemed to be a quality set (wood butcher block) and had good chairs but one was missing. The cost for the set would be $250. As you can see it can be time consuming to look around and weigh the various factors based on the situation and the likely future needs in an area.

We finally went to an estate sale where they had a high quality dining set (Ficks & Reed) in rattan, with a glass top and cushioned chairs. There were a few small scratches on the glass and one of the chairs had a little of the rattan missing where someone had picked it but this could be easily repaired. The asking price was $1,200, which for a set such as this might be considered reasonable since new they can run to over $4,000. Yet, being a good steward it did not make sense to spend too much for the higher quality. That is, the extreme quality of the product was reflected in the price but was not enough to warrant the amount. The manufacturer's name and the original price new were also making the price higher than made sense for our son and daughter-in-law. But, at a much lower price the set would be a great addition and could last them a lifetime. We asked the seller if she would be willing to record an offer to consider if the set did not sell by the end of the sale. She agreed and we left an offer of $350 and said we would stop by at the end of the sale to see if it was still available. That offer was 71 percent less than what the seller was looking for but believed it was a fair price based on what could be afforded and keeping in mind what we would spend if we were to take any of the other options with their various drawbacks. If the offer were accepted they would have a beautiful dining set that could be used in many types of rooms such as a sunroom in the future and last

them a lifetime. In addition, they would have purchased something that they likely would never be able to afford at retail and would have been much less than other sets of lesser quality at a furniture store. On returning to the sale the seller accepted our offer and our son and daughter-in-law had a great dining room set at a small fraction (likely much less than 20%) of its original cost. In fact we learned recently that they were able to trade that set in for another newer set that was more practical for their home with no additional cost.

The key in dealing with sales and auctions is to be patient, be willing to make offers, and be willing to take a "no" and walk away when the price is not what you need it to be. Do not let your emotions get the best of you. We knew that if we received a "no" on our offer for the dining set that there would be many other opportunities

available in the future. It does not make sense to pay more than you are able. In fact, when we returned to the sale we made an offer of $25 for two stools (priced at $150) that matched the dining set but the owner wanted $50. We walked away from it because we did not want to spend more than what we felt we could offer for them and based on the other factors we have noted.

Church Community. Another way to reduce the cost of items is by sharing together as a church community. This may include buying items in bulk together or working together to accomplish various tasks. For example, we have already noted having a car repair day where those in the local church who are experienced in car repair invite the brothers and sisters to bring their vehicles to them for auto maintenance or repair at a reduced cost or for the cost of materials. The same could be done for cleaning, painting, home repair, and the like. In order for this kind of thing to be successful individuals must be willing to communicate about their needs so that the appropriate efforts are made.

Along the same line is renting items together for major projects and splitting the cost. Quite often it is more economical to rent power washers, compressors, log splitters, and the like rather than buying them. Perhaps more than one church member has the same need and they can share the cost of renting the equipment.

Thrift Stores. Do not forget the savings available by shopping at thrift stores. In addition, these often use the proceeds of their sales to help individuals in the community. Examples include the Salvation Army, Goodwill, and Habitat for Humanity. You can often secure furniture and household goods in very good condition from these stores at a deeply discounted price.

There are many ways of reducing the cost of goods purchased but it is important that you make an effort to consider how that can be done each time you purchase something. You will be amazed at the savings you will find if you total the savings on each item you purchase. Those savings can then be used to build your assets that can produce income in the future.

Other Ways to Save

There are many good ways to reduce outflows and in this section we provide some other fine ways of reducing your outlays. This does not mean there will be no cost but it could be much less.

Repairs and Upgrades – Do It Yourself (DIY). One of the largest expenses of repairs is the labor. If you can learn some basic home and auto repair you can save significantly. The Internet provides a wealth of information today on how to tackle various problems. Several years ago we had sought an estimate on having laminate flooring installed in a few rooms in our home along with carpet in the rest. The bids we were receiving were just too much for what we wanted to spend. In looking at the Internet we found the same brand of laminate flooring and using the instructions that came with it and checking for comments on the Web we installed the flooring throughout the house for less than the quote for the two rooms from the flooring store. Of course the tradeoff was our time and the speed at which the work occurred. Do not just limit it to home and car either. You might be able to repair an appliance, a tool, or computer as well. We recently repaired a tape measure to save the $9.00 it would have cost to get another and there was no additional cost except the time to take it apart and glue a part. Every little bit helps.

There is a great deal of help available if you take the time to look. In addition to repair manuals and books, courses in the community, and experienced friends, there are many good helps on the Web. Some sites include: DoItYourself.com, AutoZone, Lowes, Expert Village, MonkeySee, and DIY Network. Use a search engine to deal with specific computer problems or errors as there are many forums to get help. Some include MaximumPC, TechGuy, and CompuForums, among many others. See the Web resource list at the end of the book for a listing of these Web sites. You can also search for help in repairing other items as well such as bikes and appliances. Google and Usenet also have newsgroups that deal with do-it-yourself projects and repair.

Cherry-Picking. Cherry-picking is the term used to identify those who go to multiple stores to shop in order to get the best sales. Thus, the purpose would be to go to multiple grocery stores and pick up the sale items to save money. Although many have thought that such actions were not cost effective recent research by Hoch and Fox seems to suggest that these individuals do indeed save significantly up to $17.45 a day compared to $8.68 for those loyal to a single store. The lesson is that if you plan your route carefully and stores are reasonably close together that you can save significantly by only buying sale items at different stores. Stores that are close together will also have more competitive pricing for items reducing your costs.

Store-Loyalty Cards. Along with the previous point it is beneficial to get the store loyalty cards even if you are not very loyal. These will allow you to get the sale price on items in the stores that have such cards. Some stores will also send you coupons based on what you buy in the store which can also be of help.

Product Location. Remember that product location in retail (especially grocery) stores is important. The most expensive items are usually put within easy reach and view (at eye level or on the end of the isles). Look for better prices outside of these locations. Sometimes the end of aisles are mixed with sale and non-sale items so be careful.

Economies of Scale. Usually larger packages of items have a lower per unit cost but this is not always the case. Check first to make sure you are getting the lowest per unit cost. It may not be worth buying larger, even if the per unit cost is lower, if you do not use the entire product or share it with another. Also, usually the more you buy of an item the lower the per-unit cost but again it is best to verify.

Errors at Checkout. Shoppers regularly find errors at the checkout on pricing. We recently had this happen when we were buying some candy that was on sale. Using the self-checkout the price came up 2.5 times what we expected because the sale price was not in the computer. The clerk fixed the error and we received the first candy product for free. Some stores will give you an item for free if the pricing is incorrect. Of course you may find an error in the store's favor as well. We recently purchased some items including a greeting card at Target and we looked at the receipt before we left. The clerk had failed to charge us for the card so we went over to customer service and paid for it. Though it cost us more rather than less, our Christian testimony was important.

Manufacturer Sites. If we are looking to purchase an item we will often check the manufacturer's Web site to see if there is a coupon for it. You may also find rebates at these sites. Also, by signing up to get emails you may get special discounts and promotions. Use one of the free emails such as Yahoo! or Google to avoid cluttering your main email box. There also may be Internet only specials being run and can you can look at weekly ads without having to purchase a newspaper. You can easily find a store using iStorez.com.

> "Another way to reduce the cost of items is by sharing together as a church community."

You can also signup for RSS (Really Simple Syndication) feeds at manufacturer Web sites so that they can send news about promotions to your PC for you to browse. You'll need an RSS reader (such as Internet Explorer from Microsoft or other product such as FeedReader). Some stores such as Sears provide "widgets" which can be downloaded and installed as icons on your desktop. By clicking on the icon you will see the store's promotions and specials.

Vacation Swaps. Vacations can be quite expensive and one way of reducing that cost is to eliminate the cost of the place to stay. The Internet has provided new avenues to make this a reality. There are several sites now available that allow you to swap your home with somebody else. This not only saves the cost of a hotel but since you will have another's home to use you will have a kitchen and other functions of the home that can save on eating and entertainment costs. The savings can be significant. Some sites to visit include HomeExchange. com, HomeLink International, Intervac, and Digsville. There is a fee for using these sites to swap.

One-stop Shopping. Be careful not to try to buy everything at the same place. Although you may save some gas money you may spend more than the savings by trying to get everything in one place. Plan your shopping carefully so you can go to several stores that are close together. Non-food items in grocery stores are often more expensive than discount stores so be sure to check before buying. You can also use shopping "bots" to find stores that sell what you are looking for. Some of these include PriceGrabber, MySimon, NexTag, and BizRate.

Price Guarantees. Many stores have a low price guarantee to encourage you to buy at their store. It's a nice selling point as people often think that to have such a statement they must have the lowest prices and so may not check. Many also give you 30 days to find a lower price. Check store Web sites and ads to see if you can find a lower price for the same item and the store where you purchased the item will refund the difference and perhaps add 10% to it. Several Web sites that can be helpful in letting you know about price changes for products include Price Protectr and RefundPlease.

Shipping Costs. The price of mail and shipping continues to go up. Whether you are doing the mailing or you are buying something to be shipped you should seek ways to minimize the cost. Using the U.S. Postal Service Shipping Assistant software that installs on your computer can save some money and time when you ship. If you ship frequently getting an online account at most of the major shippers will help you to save at least 10 percent. Looking for free shipping at vendor sites or finding a promotional code for free shipping can also be helpful when purchasing items. Some stores allow you to order online and then get free in-store pickup. This is great for heavy items that would normally cost more for shipping than the item itself. We recently purchased some water softener pellets from Ace Hardware. For 3 bags it would have been over $50 for shipping but we were able to pick them up at the local store with no shipping charge.

Managing Outflows to Liabilities and Others

Loan and Debt Payments

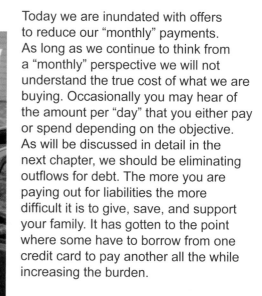

Today we are inundated with offers to reduce our "monthly" payments. As long as we continue to think from a "monthly" perspective we will not understand the true cost of what we are buying. Occasionally you may hear of the amount per "day" that you either pay or spend depending on the objective. As will be discussed in detail in the next chapter, we should be eliminating outflows for debt. The more you are paying out for liabilities the more difficult it is to give, save, and support your family. It has gotten to the point where some have to borrow from one credit card to pay another all the while increasing the burden.

It is difficult to get rid of all liabilities. For instance, annual tax bills are still something that must be paid. Outside of that type of liability (which can be seen as an annual expense) all debt and loans should be paid off as quickly as possible. We realize there will be arguments related to the low interest rates and the tax benefits of home equity loans and the like. Forget them. Get your debt paid off. There is more than just the interest rate and taxes involved in most financial decisions. We will discuss the Christian's view of taxes in a later chapter. Your goal is to have your funds, as a steward, flowing into the asset column, not the liability column. Assets can generate additional income, liabilities do not.

The Home and Car as Liabilities

As we have already noted in the text, the home and car are viewed as assets from an accountant's perspective. From a steward's perspective we need to view them differently. That is, for the steward they become liabilities. Our thinking has been colored by the world's view. It sees houses and sometimes cars as investments that appreciate in value. In reality, homes can, and cars will, depreciate in value. In addition, the cost of maintaining these purchases is huge and thus, any idea that they are an investment is lost. How many of us would be willing to spend an amount maintaining an investment portfolio equal to what we spend on maintaining our homes or cars? Few would take up the idea.

Assets generate income and this is why in a previous chapter we emphasized the steward moving the home and car from the asset column to the liability column.

Homes and cars are not investments because they do not generate any income. Now you may raise a flag and say, "wait a minute, the value of our house has gone way up so it should be seen as an investment!" Is the purpose of your home to generate that value or for a place to live? That is, any value created by owning a home is secondary to the purpose of having the home – a place to live. In fact, it should not matter whether it goes up or down in value since its purpose is not for investment but for living in. To see a home as an investment we must be willing to relinquish it at any time. Let's say to tap the value of your home you take out a loan and invest the proceeds. You use the income from the investment to help pay the new loan. What happens if the market tumbles and you lose most of the value of your investment or at least enough to make it so that you are unable to repay the loan? Now what will you do? If you do not find a way to keep up the payments the bank will foreclose on your "investment." Where will you live then? See, the world has us thinking the wrong way, and from a biblical perspective we need to be good stewards and provide for our families. The world's thinking is do not worry about being a steward you deserve all that you can get and if you lose it then others (such as the government) should provide for you and your family.

Although we will continue, for accounting purposes, to keep our cars and homes in the asset column let's continue to view them as liabilities. As a result our goal is to pay them off and keep the expenses to maintain them to a minimum so that we are able to keep them for what they are intended – a place to live and a way to get from one place to another. The stories are numerous of those who have seen them as investments and as a result lost them as an investment and had no place to live or a way of getting from one place to another. Commit now not to put yourself or your loved ones in that situation.

Gifts

We have already noted that Christmas gift buying is quite often a silent budget buster. Because of the excitement and fanfare of this time of year as well as our natural desire to show love for those in our family we likely will overspend. As with other areas of spending we need to have a plan or list of what gifts will be purchased for whom. We need also to keep in mind our list of questions when considering such an expense especially whether there is a way of reducing the cost.

In addition to Christmas, there are many other events throughout the year that will occur that may result in the spending of resources for gifts. These include birthdays, anniversaries, weddings, and the like. You need to plan these ahead and see if there are ways of reducing the cost such as by making your own gifts or using some of the other savings ideas noted in this book. It truly is the thought that counts and the goal should be to express that love without overspending or going into debt.

Keep in mind there may be gift collections at work for various individuals when they retire, have birthdays or leave for a new position. Although you may want to help, be careful to budget wisely. If you cannot afford to give then make a little something and create a card by hand to give rather than giving cash as others do.

The point to note here is that many individuals and families do not realize how much they end up spending on gifts and cards until they begin to keep track of it. After they do they are amazed by the sum they have spent. This is because the giving occurs throughout the year and thus is spread out in small amounts. When they are added together they become very large.

Exercises and Research Activities

1. You have decided to purchase a cell phone plan for $40 a month. Assuming no inflation and an interest rate of 7% how much will the phone have cost you after 40 years?

2. You have decided to buy a new 10 mega-pixel digital camera. Do some research and find the lowest price you can pay for it. Write a report that identifies where you checked and the steps you took in trying to reduce the price to the absolute minimum.

3. Visit an auction and just watch what occurs. Create a brief report on what ways you thought individuals were doing well and ways in which they overspent and why.

4. Create a complete list of all the gifts and cards you usually buy in a year. Include all friends, relatives, fellow-workers, and your church community. Try to identify how much you would spend over the year and then comment on the results.

5. You currently own your home debt free but a buddy has just heard about a great deal on a home equity loan that will give you cash for a vacation and the interest on the loan is tax deductible. What would you do and why?

CHAPTER 6

Managing Credit, Borrowing, and Debt

Learning Objectives

1. Understand and explain the beginnings of credit.

2. Explain the biblical perspective on borrowing, debt, and surety, and how they differ.

3. Discuss the advantages and disadvantages of credit cards.

4. Explain the biblical view of bankruptcy.

Lord, I commit to being debt-free.

Lord, I know you are able to provide for my needs. Help me to not rush into large purchases that will cause me to have a different ruler other than you in my life. I commit now to become and stay debt-free. By your Spirit guide me in taking the right steps to eliminate any debt I currently owe and to begin to build assets that I can use to make the major purchases that may be necessary in the future. It is only with your help that I can make this a reality so I put my confidence in you.

The Beginnings of Credit

The Basics of Credit

Credit comes from the Latin "credere" meaning to trust, loan, believe. The idea being that one could be trusted to return or repay that which he has borrowed. Today we see it as the capacity to borrow based on our ability to repay. That is, we are deemed trustworthy and able to repay. If we have no source of income and wish to borrow money the bank will not lend it since they do not trust that we can repay it. Even if we have the ability to repay the funds, if the bank finds that we have gone bankrupt or have not been consistent in paying our bills they will not consider us to be "trustworthy" and may deny us the opportunity to borrow.

Where did the idea of credit come from in the first place? Credit likely started as a small thing but has mushroomed into a multi-billion dollar business for banks. The parable of the talents shows that even in New Testament times there were bankers who could take your money at interest (Matthew 25:27). It was likely that they would then trade with the money in hopes of making a profit on it greater than the amount that they had to pay out in interest.

Credit likely was born out of the economic process. Let's see how that might have occurred. Larry Burkett, in his book *Your Finances in Changing Times* gives an excellent example how this may have developed and we will paraphrase the idea here using corn instead of nails as he does. Let's say we grow corn to swap for goods or sell for money. The recipients of our payment of corn may not need it right now so they ask us to keep it for them. This works fine for a while and we actually end up with a surplus owned by others because they have paid for it but they do not have the room to store all of it. As they need some corn they can come and get it. Others continue to buy it as needed. One day someone comes and wants to buy some corn but cannot pay until his next paycheck comes in. This gives us a great idea. We can lend some of the corn others have left with us to the individual and charge a little extra (interest) for the risk that we are taking. So, easily, the economy has now begun to work on credit. In fact, word gets around to others that we are willing to help in this way and pretty soon we have become corn bankers. As long as we have enough corn to cover the amounts requested by those who own it, the system works fine.

What happens if someone comes and wants all of his corn and we do not have enough to cover the request until we buy some elsewhere or until the next harvest? Just as fast as the word got around about our willingness to lend, the word gets around that we cannot pay back what is owed. Individuals quickly lose confidence in us and soon we are forced to close our operation in bankruptcy. What happened? Credit seemed to be so attractive and it helped others but eventually led to the downfall of the business. The problem is that credit looks and behaves like money. You can save it, divide it, sell it, and give it to others and yet it lacks one key thing – it has no tangible value. That is, we can create credit without it costing us anything. See, it goes back to our definition – the ability to repay or to be trusted to repay. In the credit scenario no additional value is attached. We are just lending what belongs to another. We can store what belongs to another and we can divide it into portions and give it to others, and we can sell what belongs to another but that does not change the fact that it costs you nothing to do so. Another way of looking at it is that there is no corresponding component created that backs up the "corn" that was lent so when the individual that owns the corn wants it, you must get it from another or create more.

Similarly in our banking system today we have money instead of corn. Many individuals put funds in the bank for safekeeping. As individuals need access to their funds the bank gives it to them. Now in this scenario the bank desires that you deposit funds with them so they do give you interest on your funds. Thus, there is some cost related to banking as we know it but this is more than recouped by the bank in lending out your funds to others at higher interest. Just like with the corn. The bank does not keep all of your money in one place doing nothing. It uses it to generate revenue through interest on the funds it lends to others. The system is fine as long as everyone does not request his or her money all at once. Why? Because the credit does not create any additional value in terms of real money. Knowing that money deposited in the bank is usually more than is requested from the bank allows the bank to lend much more than they receive. Thus, the money you deposit at the bank is not really there, it is "virtual." When you want it the bank will either take it out of what cash reserves it does have or borrow it. To you it is no different than if it were your money specifically, as long as you get the money when you request it. It is when a request is denied that panic sets in and confidence in the system causes it to collapse much like it did around 1930.

What many do not realize is that credit (the ability to repay what is borrowed) has also made the value of some items quite expensive. Homes for instance would likely be much less expensive if credit was not available. The author remembers his grandfather bought a house in 1945 for $4,500. At the time 15-year mortgages with up to 40 percent down were the standard. As banks changed the standard to allow longer borrowing periods the number of individuals who could afford a home increased. This, of course, increased competition for the supply of houses and that caused the values to go up. Now mortgages are available for up to forty years and few people ever pay their home off. The same has occurred with automobiles. Loans that at one time would be for a year or two now are for seven years or more. Few people ever pay off their cars before getting another.

In summary, credit is the capacity to borrow, and implied in that word is the confidence that you can repay what is owed. It allows an individual to buy that which currently would financially be out of reach. In the American economy credit started out as a way of helping folks who had real needs and could be trusted to repay but quickly mushroomed into a way of getting money for most any purpose and for extremely long periods of time. As a result many borrowed to speculate with investments and unfortunately many have lost (1930s) and continue to lose all that they have. An important lesson in credit is that we need to have the ability to repay. Credit can be helpful in buying expensive items such as homes but it must be carefully considered in light of the entire financial plan.

The Biblical Perspective on Credit

The Biblical View of Borrowing and Debt

Now that we have defined credit and how it is tracked in our society the question becomes whether the Christian should borrow or be in debt. Well, for an answer to this question we most go to the Bible. As we look at the Scriptures in their entirety we find first that borrowing is a valid biblical principle and second that it is different from debt. Starting in the Old Testament we see borrowing first noted in Exodus 22:14. "If a man borrows anything from his neighbor and it is injured or dies while its owner is not with it he shall make full restitution." We learn two things from this verse, first, that borrowing is allowed and second that it must be repaid. Whether its animals, equipment, or money we are to repay anything we borrow – that is the biblical principle. Psalms 37:21 reinforces this point "The wicked borrows and does not repay."

Often we will be asked about the verse in Romans 13:8 that states to "owe no man anything." Does this mean we cannot borrow? As we have already noted it is clear that borrowing is allowed but what is often missed is what is meant by "owe." That is, debt is different from borrowing. In English our term "owe" is quite broad and includes those who regularly repay what they have borrowed. From a biblical perspective one is not considered to be in debt or "owing" until he has not met his obligation to pay. That is, he is not in debt until he breaks the vow to repay at the appointed time in the appointed manner. So in Romans 13 it is showing that our love will be constrained by priorities to others we have broken vows to. If we are repaying what we have vowed to repay then we are free to love. He who does not repay his vow enters a state of being in debt and is focused on that position rather than that of being able to love. The owing becomes one of not having paid what is supposed to be paid rather than the

issue of borrowing. Thus, biblical debt and borrowing are different things.

So far then, we have seen that borrowing was allowed by the Bible and that one is not in a state of debt or owing, biblically speaking, until they have missed paying as agreed. On the other hand we need to note that generally borrowing is not seen as a positive thing in the Bible. That is, although the Bible allows borrowing, it never encourages it. Rather, often the comments concerning borrowing discourage the practice. Proverbs notes that "the rich ruleth over the poor, and the borrower is servant to the lender" (22:7, KJV). Concerning Israel the Lord said "Thou shalt lend to many nations, but thou shalt not borrow, and thou shalt reign over many nations, but they shall not reign over thee" (Deuteronomy 15:6, KJV). What the Bible shows us about borrowing is that the position that is assumed by the borrower is not good. Time and time again experience proves the Bible's correctness on this point. The borrower is put into a place of bondage. The terms are always in the lender's favor so that they will be assured of being repaid. This puts the borrower in the position of submission to whatever the whims of the lender might be. In many ways the amount of borrowing becomes a hindrance to what you would really like to do in life – even if it is something that God would want you to do. In a sense borrowing makes you a slave until you have repaid the borrowed amount. Is it not interesting that we often look at those who have paid all their debts as those who are "free?"

To summarize, then, the question of whether to borrow is not a question of whether it is biblical (it is allowed) but what will be your state once undertaken, and for how long will that state remain. We should avoid borrowing, if at all possible, since borrowing often leads to debt (owing) and debt leads to slavery to the lender. We are to be bondservants of Christ and not to a worldly lender. Make a commitment now to avoid the world's ways of living off other people's money by borrowing. The world views this as smart finance and a way to freedom, but the Bible views it as foolishness that leads to bondage. This does not mean that you will not find a few in this world that become financially rich off of such tactics. The issue is not one of whether it works or feels right but whether it is biblical. Commit to taking the biblical road.

"The issue is not one of whether it works or feels right but whether it is biblical."

The Biblical View of Surety

Perhaps you have not heard of the word "surety" before. It means to pledge to repay that which you have no certain way of repaying. Often this means pledging to repay on behalf of another.

This includes the common practice of cosigning for another. Let's look at what the Bible has to say about it:

"My son, if thou be surety for your friend, if thou hast stricken thy hand with a stranger, thou art snared with the words of thy mouth, thou art taken with thy words of thy mouth, do this now, my son, and deliver thyself" (Proverbs 6:1-3, KJV).

"He that is surety for a stranger shall smart for it, and he that hateth suretiship is sure" (Proverbs 11:15, KJV).

"A man void of understanding striketh hands, and becometh surety in the presence of his friend" (Proverbs 17:18, KJV).

"Be not thou one of them that strike hands, or of them that are sureties for debts. If thou hast nothing to pay, why should he take away thy bed from under thee?" (Proverbs 22:26-27, KJV).

Any questions? This should make it quite clear that any idea of pledging on behalf of others, or borrowing for that which we have no way of repaying, is not biblical. We believe that this includes pledging for family members as well. The only viable way of borrowing is to borrow on collateral. That is, if you are unable to pay, the creditor receives the item that you put up as collateral and the obligation ends. Collateral is what you pledge as payment if you are unable to repay. Often this is done with homes and cars. So, if you are unable to make the payments the creditor receives the home or car as payment and the debtor is considered free of the obligation. Be aware that some loans now also require you to pay the difference between what the bank gets in selling the collateral and what you had owed the bank. In order to stay clear of surety in these situations work with a lender who will give you a strictly collateralized loan or be sure that the value of the collateral is worth more than the amount owed on the loan. This may mean making a larger down payment on an item.

It is perhaps needless to say that many have experienced much heartache from eschewing the biblical mandate against surety. Countless are the sad events that have surrounded family members and friends who have pledged to pay for one another's loans only to find the family member or friend unable to pay and then finding themselves fully responsible for the debt incurred by the other. In addition, the repaying of that debt quite often has no return for the pledger since the item purchased is often of little value or has been repossessed. The legacy of broken families and friendships that have resulted from apparent well-meaning help in reality demonstrates that to pledge for another is no help at all and often robs the ones being pledged for the opportunity to use sound financial planning, careful seeking of God's will, and discipline in reaching goals. Keep in mind that 50% of all cosigned arrangements fail. There is a reason that the bank wants a cosigner – because they have a concern

that the borrowers will not be able to repay. If the bank is unwilling to take a risk why should you?

The question may be asked if one can undertake a cosign recognizing that he has the funds saved in the bank to repay if the borrower is unable to. The purpose would be to help a child or young person to learn about paying back a loan and build credit. This we must leave between the individual and the Lord. The fact that the individual understands the situation and is not in a surety situation if the borrower cannot repay is certainly better. Keep in mind though relationships can still be strained by unexpected results.

Our lesson in this section shows us that although borrowing is biblical it puts the borrower in a poor position of being a slave to the lender when he is unable to repay. Our common practice today of pledging or cosigning for others for the most part encourages unscriptural borrowing and puts the Christian in a bondman's position until the loan has been paid. Biblical borrowing always involves having a way of repaying which means using proper loan instruments, worthwhile collateral, and appropriate down payments. Having nothing borrowed truly makes you free to serve the Lord.

The Use and Abuse of Credit Cards

Today, financial institutions provide a variety of credit vehicles using cards. These can be divided into three main groups. The most common are credit cards. These have a "line of credit" pre-established based on your credit worthiness. Credit cards are often called revolving credit accounts because the credit line cycles up and down based on what you charge or pay. Thus, a $50 payment will in a sense revolve to $50 more (minus interest and fees) available on your credit limit. These accounts require a minimum monthly payment, which is usually a small portion of the outstanding balance on the

account. A second type of card is a "charge card." This type of card may or may not have a credit limit although most theoretically do even if there is none stated. The key difference is that the full balance of the account is due each month. Thus, the funds are usually borrowed for brief periods until the next billing statement comes and the payment is made. A third type of card is the "debit card." These cards usually deduct money directly from your bank account as if you were paying cash. Although they are not usually sources of credit, some debit cards can also function as credit cards, but the funds are eventually taken from your account. Using the card for this purpose is the same as using a standard credit card. ATM or bank cards at times can function as credit or debit cards.

The question will be raised as to whether it is necessary in today's society to have a credit card, perhaps for emergencies or for places that do not accept cash or checks. The answer is generally no, it is not necessary. With careful planning one can avoid having to use credit cards. We are not saying that they are not convenient but that does not mean they are necessary. There are some companies such as certain rental car companies that require a credit card. So without credit cards your rental car choices would be more limited but it would not stop you from being able to rent a car.

Exhibit 6-1 shows a list of advantages and disadvantages of credit cards with the key ones being detailed in the following discussion. There are some advantages to using credit cards judiciously. First, as noted they are quite convenient. They are easy to carry and use, and can be handy in an emergency situation.

Credit Cards	
Advantages	Disadvantages
Convenience	Overspending
Discount/reward programs	Habit leading to debt
Safety	Finance charges/fees
Merchant transaction liability	Terms favor the lender

Exhibit 6-1. Advantages and Disadvantages of Credit Cards.

Of course using a check of some kind is only slightly less convenient but a debit card is another convenient way of having this benefit. Second they can be better than carrying large amounts of cash. Of course, careful planning and the use of debit cards, checks, or money orders can mitigate this advantage. They sometimes extend the warranty on purchases made with the card. This can be helpful for some purchases such as laptop computers where a repair might be more likely but

records show that few of these warranties are ever used – that's why the company offers it as a free feature and yet few consumers will even remember that the warranty was extended even if they needed it. Unless you carefully record the information about warranties and the extension date it is likely to be forgotten. One benefit that can be quite good is that if there is any problem with the product most credit card companies will credit your account for the amount and deal with the vendor on your behalf. We remember purchasing a nice sofa at a great price a week before a company went bankrupt. Of course, they had not delivered our sofa and we had no way of getting it since the company was in bankruptcy. Since we had used a credit card we were able to get a full refund of the purchase price from the credit card company. Use of debit cards as "credit" also provides this protection. The last benefit often noted is the reward programs and the "points" you can accrue toward free or reduced price goods and services. Many cards will give you a point for every dollar (perhaps more in certain cases) you spend using the card. Keep in mind that these programs are created to encourage you to spend more and as a result keep a nice balance on the card so companies can profit off you. If you are able to restrict your use of such a card to only items that you would have purchased with cash and pay it off each month then the point programs can be a benefit. In addition, by paying the balance each month you get interest-free borrowing for your purchases for a month. The individuals are few that can do it without overspending or keeping a balance on the account.

In summary, then, the biggest benefit of credit cards that cannot be replicated by using cash is the protection offered the purchaser when a product or service is not as promised or is never delivered. Otherwise the other benefits of credit cards are only effective for those who are extremely conservative in their use and can use them as if they were cash.

There are also some disadvantages to credit cards and these are usually more than enough to offset any advantage gained from them for the average person. First, credit card users spend more because the cards usually represent more than is available with cash and there are more of them. The average American who uses credit cards has 3-4 credit cards which means the average couple has 6-8 credit cards. That is far more than is necessary for any type of emergency. The motto should be the fewer the credit cards the better. What many do not realize is that those who use credit cards are not only more likely to buy something they do not need, but will spend up to 30% more on items they do need than those who use cash. Those who commit to using cash will almost always spend less because when there is no more cash they have to stop spending, so they are more likely to conserve it. Using cash is a great way of getting your spending under control.

Another disadvantage is that credit cards can be habit forming and quickly get you into debt. We have counseled individuals who in a short time have accrued $50,000 or more in credit card debt because they were unable to control themselves. The problem is that using credit cards can put you in such a situation very quickly but it can take many years to get out of it.

The reason many do not see the problem developing is that the financial institutions have made it seem so easy with the "low monthly payment." What many do not see is that low monthly payment on 5 to 8 credit cards adds up to a very large amount. In addition, as soon as you have made that the low monthly payment you likely have used the card to purchase more goods that add that amount back on the balance. Keep in mind only 60 percent of the over $100 billion charged each month on credit cards is paid back. Which means Americans' credit card debt is growing at over $40 billion a month. Only about 31% of individuals pay off the balance in full each month.

Another disadvantage is the generally exorbitant fees, and interest that are charged; especially to those who keep a balance, are late paying, or go over their credit limit. Fees can range as high as 30% on credit card balances. That is, it costs you $30 a year to borrow $100. Only the bank makes out in this scenario. Most institutions charge $35 or more for being late with a payment or over the credit limit even though it costs the bank little if anything to let you be late or go over the limit. Remember, financial institutions are in the credit card business to make money – and that they do very well. In fact, the credit card industry made approximately $41 billion in profit in 2007.

Another important disadvantage is that the fine print is always in the bank's favor. How many of you as readers of this book and have a credit card have actually read the entire credit card agreement that you received with the card? Few do. It would behoove each reader to keep abreast of the constant changes to the agreements. They include clauses to increase the interest rate if you are late on a payment or have a fee to close the account. Some are changing how they calculate the interest, instituting minimum finance charges, or changing how they apply payments you have made, all of which are benefiting the financial institution and not you. Recent law changes have helped in these areas, but banks will find new ways to get your money.

Financial Problems

Since most financial problems result from poor planning and use of credit we will discuss some of the key ways that individuals use to deal with financial problems and emphasize the ones that make the most sense for the Christian. Keep in mind that it can take a great deal of time to get yourself out of financial difficulties and so you will need to be committed to making it happen if you are to be successful.

Debt Roll-Up or Payoff

The best way of dealing with credit problems is to deal with the root cause and then methodically pay off the outstanding balances. Usually the root cause relates to no or poor planning. The reader should go back in the book to review how to start in the area of financial planning. In addition, a debt assessment, should then be created. Based on that assessment a certain amount of funds should be set aside to reduce debt. The goal of the roll-up or payoff method is to continue to use the same level of funding to pay off debt until all are paid off. So if we start with $500 to pay off 8 credit cards each month we would continue to use that same amount even when one of the debts is paid off. This will expedite the debt payoff. When one debt is paid the payment that was going to that debt is added to one of the other debts (usually the one with the highest rate or least amount of time left). This process continues until all the debts are paid.

Debt Consolidation Loans

Whether you are still in school or well into your career you will likely receive many solicitations for debt consolidation loans. Usually the intent is to combine your various debt payments that usually involve several sources into a single monthly loan payment that you pay to a single source. Of course the purveyors of these loans make it appear that they are trying to help you to reduce the amount you are spending. In reality, in almost all cases you will end up paying more for these loans over the long run. There are usually three key benefits touted by those who market these loans that you need to carefully weigh before using them.

The Financial Benefit. All of the loan advertisements will emphasize that you will pay less each month. As with most credit today the emphasis is on the "monthly payment" with little regard to the overall cost of the entire loan. Usually the emphasis will include the reduced interest rate you will pay on the loan. Most consolidation loans are used against the home so they are more secure for the bank and thus they can offer a lower interest rate because of the reduced risk. Some credit cards will tout their transfer capabilities as a way of consolidating debt as well. In relation to any financial benefits you need to look at three questions:
What is the total cost of the debt consolidation until the

loan is paid off including any fees to initiate the loan? Most of these debt consolidation loans do not make sense in the long run as you will be paying interest on the balance for a much longer period. Second, have you dealt with the issue that got you into the current state? Many folks find it difficult to control their spending so they need to keep borrowing via credit cards. Once the payments get to be too much they consolidate them, which leaves the monthly payment lower but then they continue to use the credit cards to rack up more debt. Before undertaking any debt consolidation the root problem of spending must be dealt with first. Third, what is the interest rate? Look at the details of the offer carefully. Many times the interest rate is a very low fixed rate for an introductory period and then increases or the rate is variable based on some index that is based on the prime rate.

The Tax Benefit. Often debt consolidation loans are secured by a lien on your home. That is, they basically become a mortgage on your home. As a result the interest from the loan is considered tax deductible in some cases (although you should check to be certain). Even if the interest is deductible you may still end up paying more by taking the debt consolidation approach than by consistently paying off your debt based on a firm plan. Also, as we have noted under taxes, the standard deduction for taxes has been increasing each year making it more difficult for individuals and families to meet the threshold where itemized deductions help. If you do not have enough deductions to itemize them then the interest you pay will not be tax deductible and the benefit is useless. Also, if the loan is not secured by the home then the interest is not deductible at all.

Ease of Payment. A third benefit often touted is the ease of making a single monthly payment rather than incurring costs and taking valuable time related to mailing payments to a multitude of companies. Again there is some truth to this but the question becomes how much will the benefit cost over the long run? If you can pay your bills online for free then the savings is minimal at best and likely not enough to justify debt consolidation.

In summary, debt consolidation may occasionally be of benefit but only in very specific situations where the root problem has been dealt with and the reduced costs are demonstrable over the long term. They are normally not a benefit for those using them and usually cost much more than expected. Carefully consider other alternatives before turning to a debt consolidation loan.

Credit Counselors

Although most people might consider resolving financial problems though bankruptcy another alternative is to seek out a financial counselor who can counsel you concerning your debt. Be very careful though how you choose your counselor. There are hundreds of credit-counseling companies springing up that purportedly desire to help you but whose only goal is to make money off you. Companies whose intent is to fix your credit or only deal with your debt and not with your entire spending plan are not worth looking at. Consider checking with your local church to see if there is someone who is qualified to give good Christian counsel concerning finances. Whoever you work with should be a Christian grounded in the Word of God. You need to have a biblical perspective of finance and most of the organizations in this world will not provide that. Another possibility is to contact an organization such as Crown Financial Ministries. They keep track of trained Christian financial counselors who can be of help. You can also check with the National Foundation for Credit Counseling and the Association of Independent Consumer Credit Counseling Agencies for qualified counselors though the members are not necessarily Christian.

Keep in mind that even with Christian counselors there may be some fee involved. Be sure to ask what, if any, fees there are. It is not wrong for the counselor to charge a fee but it should not be exorbitant and should be within your ability to pay. Anyone requiring a large up-front fee should be avoided.

Debt Settlement Services

Some firms offer to settle your debts for substantially less than the current balances. Be very careful. Many of the claims can be exaggerated. There is little doubt that your credit score will be adversely affected by using a debt settlement approach. Avoid firms that require upfront or set up fees or have large ongoing costs. You actually can work with many of your creditors yourself to reach a settlement for an account as well and avoid the fees. See if you can also get the company to report that your account was paid as agreed to the credit bureaus which will be better for your credit report. Be sure to get everything in writing before sending in any payments to settle an account. Do not use firms that do not deal with the root problem (usually related to no planning).

The Biblical View of Bankruptcy

Since we are dealing with credit and borrowing in this chapter it seems appropriate to take a moment here to cover the topic of bankruptcy. The term bankruptcy means that an individual is in a state where he is unable to meet his financial obligations or the legitimate claims against him. Often the term "insolvency" is applied which means the inability to pay just debts. Federal law has made it almost appear that bankruptcy is a normal part of life and many see it as a viable way of freeing oneself from financial debts that were the result of poor decisions. Americans have taken advantage of this to file record numbers of bankruptcies in an effort to easily get rid of debt. Is this the biblical perspective? Interestingly, the government now recognizes that many have abused the law and bankruptcy law was recently updated to make it more difficult to get rid of debt without paying it. These changes took effect in October, 2005.

It is a sad commentary to note the number of Christians taking advantage of the bankruptcy law today. Just because something is legal does not mean it is biblical. Prostitution may be legal in some states but it does not make it biblical. The biblical mandate is to repay what you owe. It is clear that those who borrow and do not repay are counted among the wicked (Psalms 37:21). How is it that Christians are so quick to be numbered with the wicked? The key is man's wisdom. That is, Christians rationalize that bankruptcy is a legal way that God has provided through the government to deal with a difficult situation and perhaps will go as far as to say that it provides a blessing to have it available. See how far rationalization will take you? To see something that is wicked as a blessing? See, human logic tries to find ways around the position that we have put ourselves in by poor financial planning.

The biblical perspective of bankruptcy is that we repay our just debts. It is important here to note "just" debts. These are debts that you have promised to repay for which the borrower has not accepted some form of payment. If you can meet with your lenders and get them to reduce your payments, interest rates, or to take something less or different than what was agreed on, then that is biblical. As long you and the lender can work out an agreement then you are abiding by the biblical standard. Luke 12:58-59 notes: "for as thou goest with thine adverse party before a magistrate, strive in the way to be reconciled with him, lest he drag thee away to the judge, and the judge shall deliver thee to the officer, and the officer cast thee into prison. I say unto thee, thou shalt in no wise come out thence until thou hast paid the very last mite" (JND).

It is possible that your creditors will force you into bankruptcy. That is something that they, by law, can do. By doing so they are accepting as payment whatever the court allows. The Christian does not initiate the bankruptcy because of financial mismanagement but seeks in every way to repay what is owed by working with the lenders. Once the lender takes action by law to accept whatever the court gives as payment then the Christian is no longer obligated to pay anything since the lender has agreed to accept what the court gives as payment in full for the outstanding debt. The problem is when the Christian initiates the bankruptcy. This forces the lender to accept as payment what the court gives and does not "biblically" absolve you of the need to repay the difference. Remember, when borrowing the lender becomes the master and must be the one that chooses whether an alternative payment is acceptable. Your forcing an unacceptable payment through bankruptcy does not free you from making up the difference to the lender so that the payment is acceptable.

It is possible with our litigious age in this country that you may be served with an unjust financial judgment. There are many in society who make a living by finding ways of suing another or who look for any way of making a financial gain of the smallest accident. This could be a financial award to another party for something that you had no involvement in or an award that far exceeds the repayment of whatever injury you caused. In these types of rare situations the Christian may have no other choice but to file for bankruptcy in order to lessen the burden of the unjust judgment. This is the only reason (an unjust debt) that we can think of currently, that would provide the Christian a basis for filing for bankruptcy.

Exercises and Research Activities

1. Secure a copy of your credit report and review it. Write a brief review and identify any errors in the report and the steps you will take to correct them. What can you do to improve your credit score if you so desire?

2. What does it mean in Romans when it speaks of "owing no man anything"?

3. Write a brief abstract on what surety is and its advantages and disadvantages. Explain why the Bible is so against it.

4. Research a story about the abuse of credit cards and the results of that abuse. Write a brief paper about the story and what we can learn from it.

5. You have just arrived in the area and would like to secure a credit card. Research the possibilities and choose a card based on all of the relevant characteristics of a credit card. Write a brief abstract that identifies your top two choices and how they are better than others. Include a table that compares the features you were looking at.

CHAPTER 7

Making Major Purchases — Home, Car, and Education

Learning Objectives

1. Identify the appropriate steps in purchasing a home or car.

2. Discuss the tradeoffs of securing student loans for education and what other means may be available for securing an education.

3. Explain how other major purchases such as appliances, weddings, and furniture should be accomplished.

Lord, I commit to planning major purchases.

Lord, thank you for your wisdom concerning credit and its use and abuse. Please help me to plan the major purchases in life carefully. I desire to be your servant and not a slave to a lender or to things. Help me to save as needed so I can be ready to make the major purchases in life that will come along. I promise to count the cost of any borrowing carefully before undertaking it. Thank you again for your strength and support.

Making Major Purchase Decisions — Home, Car, and Education

Most financial planning books provide a good review of what is involved in purchasing a home and car so we will not cover the details of those in this chapter other than to give a summary of a plan for doing so. Here we will look at a few other areas involving major purchases often overlooked.

Providing for a Home or a Car

If there is one area that Christians have followed the world's lead, it is in how they buy homes and cars. Americans, rather than looking at these items for what they are intended (the automobile as a form of transportation and the home as a shelter), now view them as status symbols or as investments. By viewing these assets from this perspective we also view the amount we spend differently. If we see our car as a home on wheels we certainly cannot go without individually controlled, comfortable leather sets, or without the state of the art surround sound system, oh, and do not forget the DVD system for the kids and while you are at it you might want to install a refrigerator for those drinks and snacks you might need. See, before we know it we can rationalize spending thousands more on a vehicle just by how we view it. For the Christian the issues of having a car or home for a status symbol should never come to mind since we are not of this world. So the idea that a Christian needs a Mercedes or Lexus to show God's blessing is ludicrous (though many preachers of the gospel drive them, sad to say). The Christian recognizes that his blessings are spiritual, as he is seated in the heveanlies with Christ (Ephesians 2:6). Even if you spend many hours in your vehicle are all of the accoutrements that dealers try to sell, necessary? Probably not.

With that as an introduction the key steps to buying a home or car are as follows:

Establish the Need. It is easy to let wants and desires influence your buying decision. Usually the result is a more expensive home or car than is required for our needs. For instance when considering the purchase of a car, if public transportation is available consider the tradeoffs of cost, time, and convenience of using that mode of transportation. Based on those tradeoffs if you determine that you need to buy a car then make sure you list what you need in a vehicle. Will you need to carry goods or many passengers? Do you need to be able to tow a trailer? Will it be used for work, and if so, what type? Answering questions like these will help you to identify the type of vehicle you will need.

The American public has been brainwashed into the idea that it is a good idea to get a new car every two to three years or to upgrade the size of their homes every five years. This is great for the realtors, dealers, and manufacturers but of little value to the people buying them. Purchase a good home or vehicle and plan on sticking with it for as long as it meets your needs. In addition, if a car is meeting the needs then it should be kept as long as it is safe to drive, and is less expensive to maintain than replacing it. A car almost always costs less in the long run to repair than to replace.

Funding. Carefully consider how you will fund your purchase. If at all possible pay cash for your purchase. When borrowing people generally buy more than they need and as a result pay more in recurring costs to maintain them. If you decide to pay cash you are much more likely to be careful to conserve it because you already have it and might want to use some of it for other things. Consider beginning to save now for purchasing a home or vehicle in the future. If you currently have no car payment, consider making the equivalent of a car payment to a savings instrument so that you will have cash to pay when you are ready to purchase your next vehicle.

Research. You must research the market carefully to see what ways would be best to fill your need. This includes looking at a variety of tradeoffs including whether to lease or own. The Web is great tool for performing research today so take advantage of it.

Insurance and Taxes. As you look for a home or car you need to keep in mind that the selection can significantly influence your insurance and taxes.

New versus Used Cars. If you already own a car you may also have the option of repair. That is, some people who start looking for a car do so because their current vehicle requires some type of repair. Although each situation is unique the following general conclusions can be drawn. It is almost always cheaper to repair a car than buy a new one (unless you have a loved one who owns the dealership or something of that nature). In a vast number of cases it is cheaper to repair than to buy a used car. It is almost always cheaper to buy a used car than a new car. New cars are rarely a wise choice unless you plan on keeping them for many years.

With these general points in mind the Christian, as a good steward of the resources that God has given, will only consider a new car as a long term purchase that will last many years; normally ten years or more. With that in mind, if you expect, due to family changes (e.g. addition of children) to change vehicles in a shorter time frame a new car should be avoided. Most new cars lose a significant amount of value just by their being purchased and driven off of the dealer lot (sometimes as much as 25%). It makes no financial sense to be buying new cars every two or three years no matter how great the world portrays that scenario. If you do purchase a new vehicle and maintain it well for ten or more years then the per-year cost can be quite low.

Buy versus Lease on Cars. Another question often raised in the buying process is whether one should buy or lease the vehicle whether new or used. The answer is simply that it never makes financial sense for an individual or family to lease a car for personal use. There may be some tax benefits for businesses that lease vehicles but those benefits do not accrue to individuals and there are few benefits to leasing and we repeat NO LONG-TERM FINANCIAL ADVANTAGES. Considering there are no long-term financial advantages and there are many possible disadvantages the recommendation to Christians is to avoid leasing. When you lease you are basically renting the vehicle. A home lease (or rent) can be helpful to give time to save for a home. In addition, there may be opportunities to rent with an option to buy for a home with part of the rent going toward the down payment. Many see renting a home as throwing money away but again if it meets your needs and helps you reach your goals it is fine.

The Car Extras. Dealers are in business to make money and they make every attempt to get as much as they can when you are buying a car. They do this because they know that you are more likely to splurge for the extras since you are already spending a significant amount of money and the extras may not seem like all that much when compared to the total cost of your vehicle. Avoid buying the extras that a dealer will try to offer you as part of your car transaction. These include offers of rust-proofing, sealants, fabric protectors, extended warranties, service contracts, and the like. If the car is new or has been well maintained these should be unnecessary. These are great money makers for the dealers and few consumers can actually take advantage of them due to the exclusions that go with them. For the most part these are just costly extras. You would be better off investing the funds you would have spent on these so that you would have a repair fund in case you need it. The dealer knows that if you do not buy the extras when you buy the car they will have lost the opportunity to improve its profits.

Trade-in. Avoid talking about the trade-in until you have arrived at a price that is fair for the vehicle you are buying. Often the dealer will try work in the trade as part of the pricing which is almost always to the dealer's benefit.

Zero Percent Down. Realtors and dealers will often entice purchasers by emphasizing zero percent down deals. This requires the purchaser to finance the entire purchase price. This would immediately put the individual in a situation of being unable to pay off his debts if necessary since reselling the vehicle or home would not fetch the amount owed on the loan. The caveat is that some may have the funds earning interest in the bank at a rate greater than the loan. So taking advantage of the zero percent down offer seems to make sense and if they had to they could still repay the loan. This may work but it should be carefully considered in light of other alternatives. That is, usually zero-percent down deals have higher price tags or interest rates than cash or other types

of deals. Thus, to take advantage of the zero down deal sometimes requires paying a higher price. The key here is to be careful that you do not pay more for the home or car because of the deal for zero down and be sure you would be able to repay all you have promised if necessary.

Providing Education

Education is the one non-investment instrument that might be called an investment. That is, it is funded with a large initial payment over 4 or more years in hopes that the return on that investment in the form of a better career will produce a much larger return than if it were not undertaken. For some types of professions such as law or accounting there may be ongoing expenses associated with maintaining a licensure. But some consider this no different than the expenses related to managing an investment.

Research does show that on average investing in education proves quite valuable and provides increasing returns based on the level of education attained. Research shows a correlation between education and average lifetime earnings. An associate's degree will lead to an additional half million dollars of lifetime income compared with those who do not have a college degree. Attaining a bachelor's degree adds another $650,000 of income making such a degree worth about a million dollars more than not having a college degree. Adding a master's or doctorate degree also leads to higher earnings than the bachelor's degree. Keep in mind that these are average earnings and are influenced by the current employment market and the career specialty entered.

It would seem, then, that it behooves stewards to prayerfully and seriously consider what career God would have them to enter. Keep in mind that God does not have all to attain college degrees and money should not be the focus of our desire in this world. What we learn here is that God may have some to develop certain talents and skills that will lead to greater capacities to support others. He may lead others to minister as a Bible teacher or evangelist. These, of course require a spiritual gift rather than formal education. This is why many of those who taught in the New Testament were able to do so without an education. This does not mean that a Bible teacher cannot have an education but that it is not a requirement for ministering for God. The key here, as in other decisions we make, is taking a biblical approach to our decisions seeking guidance from His Word, through prayer, and the godly counsel of others.

The School Selection Process

Although in a text such as this we can only touch briefly on some of the key points in the university selection process it is important that regardless of the training or degree you wish to pursue you will need to go well beyond the thoughts here in your research. Some general points in pursuing an education include:

Commitment. As with everything relating to stewardship, education requires you to make a commitment. This means doing well in your education activities before entering college. There is much to distract young people in this world today in the form of entertainment that pleases the flesh and as a result is more enticing than the time and commitment it takes to do well in educational studies. Determine now that you will commit to doing well in whatever educational endeavor that you, by God's grace, are put into. Of course, the benefit of this can be seen in better knowledge and understanding, and improved scholarship opportunities in the future.

Perspective. Keep in mind that as a Christian you seek to find an educational opportunity that will provide you with the education and experiences necessary to succeed in your chosen field and provide an environment in which your faith can be expressed and grow. Choosing a school because it is easy or has the most activities is not likely to help you accomplish any career goals you have set. Christian schools should be given significant consideration in light of their opportunities for significant growth in the faith and the emphasis on a biblical basis for conduct.

Price. There is no question that for many the cost of schooling plays a significant role. Although the costs of higher education have increased significantly over the last two decades there are still many good values in the educational arena. Several guides are published related to schools with the best values. A few include: Kiplinger's 100 Best Values in Public Education at www.kiplinger.com/tools/colleges/ and U. S. News and World Report's America's Best Colleges at www.usnews.com. High price does not necessarily mean great education. Price often can be associated with the well known name of a school such as the Ivy League schools like Yale and Princeton or other schools such as MIT. Although some companies may look for a degree from a certain institution this rarely will be the only criteria used. Most companies look for a solid education with demonstrated work in the area of endeavor. Thus, internships, practica, projects, and co-operative experiences play a far more important role than the school attended.

The Funding of Education

Seeing that education is an important criterion for most fields of endeavor and that it can affect our earnings it is important that we find a way of funding that experience. Keep in mind to explore tax-advantaged education investments such as 529 plans or Education Savings Accounts.

Savings. Saving regularly starting at a young age will help you to be able to fund your education or that of your children. The trend of saving in America, generally, has not been good but savings rates have increased recently because of the uncertainty in the economy. Saving is one of the best options for being ready for the need. Often this can be done tax-free if it is for education.

Scholarships. Many organizations and universities offer grants or scholarships based on a variety of factors including need, ability, and a host of other demographic factors. The great benefit of these is that they do not need to be repaid. Be careful of scholarship scam services that claim they can get you thousands for just filling out a single form. There is a great deal involved in seeking and applying for scholarships. Check where you or your parents work as they may also provide these.

Tuition Reimbursement. Many employers provide tuition reimbursement for employees. If you plan on an advanced degree this may be of help. In fact you may want to seek an employer who offers such a benefit.

Student Employment. Most universities offer employment opportunities for students that allow them to pay their tuition or lead to a remission of tuition. Although tuition remission is more common for graduate level programs some undergraduate programs offer this for juniors or seniors.

Student Loans and Grants. The federal government provides a number of programs designed to support those who have a financial need for college funds. These programs are available only to those who have filed the Free Application for Federal Student Aid (FAFSA) form with the federal government. If, based on the federal formula, you qualify for need-based assistance you can then apply for it. Grants by the government such as the Pell grant do not need to be repaid. Student loans, if you qualify, are guaranteed by the federal government and there is no interest until 6 months after school is complete. Now that brings us to another concern. Biblically speaking we need to have a way to repay what we borrow. This is rarely the case for a student. What happens if for some reason you do not finish school? What happens if it takes you a year or two to find a good position? You end up with no way of being able to pay for the loan. Because of this we cannot recommend students take out student loans unless they have a certain way of repaying them either by collateralizing them or having something of value that they could sell to repay them.

No doubt as a result of the above comments current students may question how it is possible to use a student loan or get an education without one. As we have noted careful planning and saving ahead of time is required to avoid student loans. Using some of the other means noted in this section can also help. There are ways of using student loans in such a way as to have them either partially or entirely forgiven, or to receive education free. These should be researched carefully in relation to your career aspirations and the particular requirements that are necessary to qualify for these programs. Some types of student loan forgiveness may also have income tax consequences. Some possibilities include:

Joining AmeriCorps – a national service and community organization which incorporated two former organizations; Volunteers in Service to America (VISTA) and the National Civilian Community Corps (NCCC). The organization provides $4,725 per year of service to be used for student loans or education. The amount of reward can also be pro-rated for part-time service. You also receive a stipend to help with living expenses. Additional information is available at www.americorps.gov.

Joining the Peace Corps – an international service and community organization. The organization provides Perkins loan cancellation for up to 70% of the loans with 4 years of service to the organization. Deferment of other loans is available as well. The organization also provides a living allowance. For more information see www.peacecorps.gov.

Joining the United States military. There are many options for receiving an education through the military and in many cases the education is free. The options are too numerous to be covered in this text but details can be gleaned from www.military.com/education-home/.

Teaching in participating low-income area schools. Up to 100% of the Perkins student loans can be forgiven for 5 years of full-time teaching. The amount is less for fewer years of teaching. There are also various state programs that can be used as well. The American Federation of Teachers at http://www.aft.org/tools4teachers/loan-forgiveness.htm keeps a record of current programs being offered. Also view the Federal Student Aid Web site at http://studentaid.ed.gov/PORTALSWebApp/students/english/teachercancel.jsp.

Practicing law by serving in the non-profit or public interest sector. Many law schools will forgive debt for those serving in the non-profit sector or as a public defender and there may be other ways of qualifying for reduced debt. See the Equal Justice Works Web site for additional information at http://www.equaljusticeworks.org/resources/student-debt-relief/default. The American Bar Association is another good place for information at http://www.abanet.org/legalservices/sclaid/lrap/home.html.

There are also loan repayment plans for those going into medical research. For additional information, look at the National Institute of Health Web site at http://www.lrp.nih.gov/.

Those seeking healthcare positions may receive loan forgiveness or repayment from health care providers recruiting in a specific area. Consult Web sites for specific medical areas such as the American Physical Therapy Association at www.apta.org for those interested in physical therapy. In addition to the National Institute of Health noted earlier, The National Health Services Corps also provides information on loan forgiveness or repayment at http://nhsc.hrsa.gov/loanrepayment/. Another great resource for medical students is the Association of American Medical Schools at http://services.aamc.org/fed_loan_pub/index.cfm. For those in Nursing see the Health and Human Services site at http://bhpr.hrsa.gov/nursing/loanrepay.htm.

Qualifying providers of childcare may also receive student loan forgiveness. More information is available at the Federal Student Aid Web site at http://studentaid.ed.gov/PORTALSWebApp/students/english/childcare.jsp.

Qualifying government positions may also qualify for loan forgiveness or repayment. For more information see the U.S. Office of Personnel Management at http://www.opm.gov/oca/pay/studentloan/.

As the reader can see there are many opportunities related to paying for a college education or removing the burden of student loans. The student will need to do some careful career planning in order to take advantage of these opportunities and it may require some public service type work before going on to the job or career path of choice but the benefits of being debt-free afterward may be worth it. No doubt there are tradeoffs but they should be carefully considered in light of the career and financial goals.

Although we may view education as an investment we realize that we must still follow the biblical mandate of having a way of paying our just debts. That is, borrowing for the purpose of "investing" in education is treated no differently than the other borrowing we have discussed. The best way of preparing for the reality of paying for education is to plan and start early. If you do not start early it can be difficult to afford the costs of education even with the various sources of help from state and federal governments as well as the schools themselves. Lack of funding is one of the primary reasons that students do not finish their college education. With the information above students should be better prepared to deal with funding their continued education. You can find a good way to fund your education without going into debt but it will require diligent research and perhaps some initial tradeoffs to make it a reality.

Other Major Purchases

Well, we have tackled most of the major expenses that we are likely to encounter. Before we leave this area though there are a few others that you are very likely to encounter but are not normally considered.

Appliances and Furnishings

Many folks do not give much thought to appliances until there is a need to replace one. By that time, quite often, one is pressed to make a quick purchase, which inevitably leads to making poor decisions and increasing costs. We should make every effort to carefully consider appliance purchases just as with other expenses. Some key points of insight regarding acquiring appliances include:

Never Rent Them. What we mean by appliances here are the ones you use regularly in the home. You should never rent or participate in a rent-to-own for washers, dryers, TVs, stoves, refrigerators, and the like. These are losing propositions for you and a great boon to the company. We have seen some of these rent-to-own stores sometimes charge as much as 600% interest on the life of a contract. Renting a large power tool for a single day may be fine (although better to borrow from a friend) but anything you use on a regular basis should be purchased.

Do not Borrow for Them. Appliances and furnishings need to be paid with cash. To borrow for an appliance will almost always put you into, biblically, a debtor's position which means if you had to sell the appliance and/or pay the balance remaining you would not be able to. Appliances depreciate extremely quickly. We have been at auctions where very good washers and dryers go for thirty dollars each even though they originally sold for many hundreds.

Be Diligent. The best way of finding good deals on furnishings and appliances is to be watching and know the market. Watch for classified ads in the paper, or for yard sales (tag sales), moving sales, auctions, and the like. Although some folks will overprice their goods most will be looking to get rid of the merchandise and will be willing to strike a deal. In reality you can probably furnish your entire home with quality items without going to the store. Our son recently got his leather living room set for $100 at a yard sale. Certainly sounds better than $1,000 or more that it likely would cost new. We also remember a brother in the Lord purchasing a high-end sofa from Habitat for Humanity for $100. Deals can be found, it just takes patience and diligence in finding them.

Weddings

Although weddings should be joyful occasions, for many they are becoming a financial burden. Most of this is due to catering to what the world expects for a wedding celebration. The average American wedding now costs

$22,000 (which is down from $28,000 in 2007) excluding the honeymoon. This is an outrageous sum for parents or newlyweds to spend for a one-day celebration. If you must fund your own, or your child's, wedding go the simple route and carefully plan it to reduce costs yet provide a memorable time for all. Our son married less than five years ago and it was great to see how he and his fiancée carefully planned with her parents to keep costs down. Instead of a big modern church the marriage was performed in a small historical church for a nominal fee. The reception was at a community hall that was rented for $50. The food was catered by Fazoli's, which provides a great Italian buffet for less than $10 per person. Our son bought a suit that can be reused rather than a tuxedo and the list on money saving ways goes on. Although we do not know all the financial numbers we would estimate that it cost less than $2,000 for the wedding and reception. By being careful they (and her parents) are in much better financial shape than would have been the case if they sought to put on a lavish spread. If you are a parent with children (especially girls in our culture) then suggest that for every $100 they save in wedding costs they receive $25.00. Just a little incentive can go a long way.

Funerals

Although sad to consider, there is no getting away from the fact that dying today is expensive. But, just like with weddings it is not necessary to spend inordinate amounts for services related to the final arrangements related to the deceased. The average American funeral is now $6,000-$8,000. Much of this though is related to lavish spending on monuments, caskets, vaults, and other accoutrements.

Again, planning ahead will help here. Consider where you would like to be buried and consider purchasing a burial plot ahead of time. Keep in mind if you move there will be expenses related to getting your body to the burial plot. Although, it may be possible for those remaining to sell the plot and buy another where you died. Also, some funeral homes have large enough networks that they can exchange or transfer plots for you. Keep the expenses to a minimum. A simple chapel service where all can come to rejoice in the believer's home-call is the best. In fact the body of the deceased is not even needed for the memorial service. Viewing hours, or wakes as they at times are called, are really optional and can reduce the cost considerably. Perhaps setting up a time for calling hours at a local church for fellowship and encouragement would be sufficient. When the body can be immediately buried the costs are substantially reduced. The viewing of the dead is not necessary so do not feel you have to plan for it. Much of what is done today takes place by tradition and has developed into a profit-making venture for many companies.

You can still provide for the burial of a loved one for a reasonable cost in the range of $2,000 and as little as $800 based on a recent article by MSN Money. Interestingly, it is about the same as a carefully planned wedding. Do not be afraid to buck the popular trend and do that which any good steward would do. The key is to plan now so there is no rush later when you or your loved ones are likely to make poor decisions.

Exercises and Research Activities

1. You and your team have been assigned to find you a home. You have decided that you are willing to move anywhere in the 48 contiguous states and that you want to pay cash with a maximum $60,000 price plus $2,500 for closing costs. Using appropriate criteria find the best deal possible. Various factors should be researched and weighed including location, safety, general job availability, and the like. The home should have 3 bedrooms and two baths and be on at least .20 acre.

2. You have decided to borrow $80,000 for your $150,000 home in Dallas, Texas. Find the best financial deal that results in the least amount being spent in total costs to acquire and pay off the loan keeping in mind that you cannot afford more than $600 a month.

3. Jae's car, a 2001, Honda Accord LX sedan, has just blown a head gasket. The mechanic suggests that it will cost $4,400 to have it fixed. He has about $6,000 in his emergency fund. Perform an analysis and create a report that shows any comparisons you undertake and identifies what you would do.

4. You and your fiancée plan on getting married soon and now need to create a budget for the big event. Create a detailed spending plan and identify ways that the cost could be reduced if necessary. Also create a spending plan based on only having $2,500 available for everything.

5. You want to plan your child's education without having to borrow in the future. If your child is currently 9 years old with no savings what will your plan be? Do some research and write an essay on how you will reach your goal.

CHAPTER 8

Managing Your Taxes

Learning Objectives

1. Describe the biblical perspective of paying taxes to the government.

2. Identify appropriate ways of reducing taxes.

Lord, I commit to carefulness in paying taxes.

Lord, help me to be careful as I pay a portion of what you provide to those that rule over me as required. Help those that rule to use what is given for your glory as they are accountable to you as rulers for what they do. May I have been found faithful in doing what is right when dealing with the government.

Managing and Reducing Taxes

The Biblical View of Taxes

Another issue related to the outflow of financial resources is in the area of taxes. Views from Christians run the gamut on the issue of taxes. Some go as far as to say that we should not pay them. Although this will not be an entire treatise on the issue we should at least understand the basic views from a biblical basis.

On one end of the spectrum we have those who believe that as Christians we should pay taxes because not to do so would be illegal. For Christians doing something illegal would not be a viable option unless the request of the government was not biblical. For instance if the government passed a law that required us to steal from our neighbors we would not obey it since the Bible clearly is against stealing. Most folks who take this perspective use Matthew 22:15-22 as a basis for paying taxes to authorities. This is the section where Jesus answered the Pharisees concerning tribute to Caesar by replying "render unto Caesar what is Caesar's and unto God what is God's." This verse seems to point out not just that taxes would be paid but that in reality such authority to collect taxes in reality comes from God. That is why he adds "render unto God what is God's."

There are other verses that clearly show that by God's permission other kings and/or governments taxed the inhabitants. Jehoiakim taxed the land so he could pay Pharaoh (2 Kings 23:35). Daniel 11:20 speaks of a raiser of taxes being on the throne for a short while which was fulfilled by Philopator (Seleucus IV) who evidently raised taxes to pay a war-tax to Rome. 1 Samuel 8 makes it clear that if the people would have a king over them that he would have the authority to exact taxes. Despite this the people wanted the king. Even in Matthew 17:24-27 where it is clear that it is the strangers of the land that are normally taxed the Lord still pays the tax so as not to offend those who expect it.

The one difficulty for those who do pay taxes may be what the government does with the funds. Even the taxes the Lord paid when on earth we are sure were not necessarily used for what He would have them used for, but God has given the earthly authority into the hands of those in leadership in the nations. Thus, taxes you pay could end up paying for that which you believe is unscriptural. It appears the Lord's example of paying taxes should be enough to quiet our hearts on this and recognize that we are not making the decision of how the government spends the funds. Your contributing taxes does not appear to be viewed in the Bible as in any way wrong from what we can see there.

At the other end of the spectrum is another school of thought believes that taxes are unbiblical and are seen as the government stealing from the people. Since the Bible is against stealing it is thought that we should not pay taxes. Another argument is that God is sovereign and since the U. S. government is a republic and does not have a king, sovereignty to collect taxes has not been conveyed to it so it is wrong for them to collect them. Others suggest that if a government takes more than a tithe or ten percent that it is wrong or if the tax is progressive it is wrong. Most of these concerns are based on a misunderstanding of Scripture or by applying that which applies to Israel to the Christian. As we have already noted under the topic of giving, tithing was far more than ten percent and in reality was a 22-25 percent tax to fund the government of Israel from the people themselves. Keep in mind there was no earthly king at that time over Isreal. Other than the concern about how the funds are used there is little if any biblical support for not paying taxes that are due. Interestingly, the tax by Jehoiakim could be read as being progressive – "he exacted…everyone according to his estimation" (2 Kings 23:35). Most of these folks who support not paying taxes are well meaning but not well read in the Scriptures. Most of the arguments are in man's wisdom dealing with history or logic rather than with the Word of God.

Interestingly, both groups of people use the verse from Romans 13 to emphasize that God works through rulers in the nations. Those who support paying the taxes emphasize Romans 13:6-7 where it twice says to pay tribute. Those against taxes emphasize Romans 13:3-4 that speak of the rulers' purpose of avenging evil. Thus, they would limit the government's work to that area. That is, no road building, no helping the poor, no space exploration, and the like since they are not specifically mentioned in Scripture. Unfortunately, it is clear from the Bible that governments can collect taxes and that they become the stewards of those funds and the ones who will give account. That is, our being biblically disobedient because the government is being biblically disobedient and improperly spending money is wrong. The old saying "two wrongs do not make a right" is true. We cannot be held responsible for what another does when we have done the right thing and have been obedient to the Scripture and paid the taxes. Just because the government misspends or occasionally funds that which would be objectionable to us as Christians based on a biblical perspective does not seem to be a strong enough reason for being disobedient to a direct command to us to pay tribute to whom it is due.

Based on a review of the applicable Scriptures it would seem that Christians should be obedient and pay their taxes especially since the Christian's particular payments are in no way earmarked for a particularly unbiblical support area. That being said, Christians should certainly make efforts, where appropriate and biblical, to reduce the amount of the funds spent in this area. Just like with other expenses and liabilities, saving here will allow us to do more in the future. Being a Christian does not mean we have to overpay the government but we should be honest in our tax dealings as well.

How to Reduce Your Taxes

Although we do not want to spend more just for the sake of reducing taxes we do want to make every effort to be careful that we only pay what we are required to pay. First, we would unequivocally state that we want to be honest in what we report to the IRS. As Christians we want to avoid any improprieties that tarnish our testimony for Christ. We should also note that the tax law is voluminous and honest mistakes will be made by even the most well-meaning people because they are not aware of all that the law contains or may have been misinformed by another on some point. Some of these will be caught by the IRS and will need to be corrected. At other times it may not be an issue of a mistake but perhaps you receive a letter asking for verification of a deduction and you find that you have misplaced the receipt or discarded it by accident. Unfortunately, these things happen and as a result we may end up having to pay additional tax (sometimes a mistake results in a refund). It is a reminder that we should be vigilant in keeping copies of our tax returns and any documentation that supports anything reported as well as anything that we are taking a deduction for.

I mention the above because at times in our zeal to reduce our taxes we may forget to put together the appropriate documentation or we may take a tip from someone that seems to know about reducing taxes without truly understanding what it entails. That being said, there are many legitimate ways of reducing your taxes by taking a thoughtful and careful approach to your financial plan and to your tax plan. Here are some to consider:

Start early. The filing deadline is April 15th unless you have filed for an extension by that date. By waiting to the last minute you are likely to make mistakes and well may cost yourself money by overpaying your taxes or make a careless mistake that makes them lower than they should be and if caught will cause more stress to get rectified. Start in January to get your receipts and other materials together. Install tax software if you use it or download the latest forms from the IRS Web site. Even if you wait

to mail in your return you should have it completed by March 1.

Keep your receipts and records straight. Keep all your receipts throughout the year so that they will all be in one place when you need them in January. We use a large box for receipts and all receipts end up in that box whether they will be used for tax purposes or not. By doing this you can avoid missing valuable deductions that you could forget about. It is also great for when you want to return an item to the store or need a receipt for warranty purposes. You will know right away where to go.

Consider the Computer. If you have a computer at home consider keeping track of your financial matters (including taxes) by using it. There are plenty of software packages available to help with this task. Products such as *Quicken* by Intuit and *MS Money* by Microsoft are two of the most popular. Perhaps the simplest and best we have seen for its cost was *MoneyCounts* by Parsons Technology. Intuit bought it and then as you might expect it died. These software packages will also keep track of tax related items to make it easier at tax time and you can import data into the tax software from the financial package. The more popular tax software packages include *TurboTax* by Intuit, and *TaxCut* by H & R Block. You will also find specialized tax packages to help you maximize your deductions. One that is growing in popularity is *It's Deductible* from Intuit. It appears to be quite helpful in tracking and valuing household items that you give to charity. Generally people way over or under estimate the value of items they give to charity.

Take All Exemptions. Be sure to include all dependent children and others you support that meet the IRS guidelines for those considered dependents. For each dependent there is currently a $3,500 exemption, which is significant. If you share the support of a dependent then you may be able to take turns in claiming the individual as a dependent.

Contribute to a Tax-Deferred Retirement Plan. Taxes can also be reduced by legally reducing income. One of the most popular ways is by contributing to an IRA, or an employer sponsored 401K or 403B (non-profit, government). The amount you can put in and deduct is subject to various limitations based on age and income so you will want to do some research on it. Keep in mind that these funds will be taxed when they are withdrawn. Similar accounts for educational purposes can also be funded and are tax-free as long as they are used for educational expenses.

Generate Tax-Exempt Income. Another mechanism that can be used as part of your tax planning for the future is to invest in instruments whose return is tax-free, and thus, does not need to be included in your taxable income. These might include a Roth IRA or municipal bonds.

Generate Capital Gains or Dividend Income. A capital gain is the amount realized on the sale of an asset such as stocks, bonds, or real estate that exceeds the original purchase price. This income (sale price – purchase price) is currently taxed at a much lower rate than standard income. Depending on standard income, you pay long-term (investments held at least a year, otherwise it's considered ordinary income for tax purposes) capital gains tax at the rate of 0% or 15% depending on your marginal tax bracket (this is scheduled to revert to 10% or 20% in 2011). This is significantly less than the 10%-35% you would pay on normal income. Another nice thing about this is you can decide when it would be best to sell and take the gain (or loss if it has lost value).

Dividend income from stocks is also currently taxed at a lower rate, at either 0% or 15% starting in 2008 depending on the marginal tax bracket you are in. This rate is scheduled to revert to the rates on ordinary income in 2011.

Give Your Money to Others. As of 2009, you can give up to $13,000 ($26,000 with a spouse) to as many people as you care to without encountering any tax consequences. This limit is adjusted for inflation each year. The person receiving the gift does not have to pay taxes on the gift either. What is nice about this option, as well, is if the individual receiving the gift is in a lower marginal tax bracket then any income he earns on the gift will be taxed at a lower rate than if you had been taxed on the income from it. This in particular is a nice way for relatives and brethren in Christ to share the wealth.

Exercises and Research Activities

1. Write a short essay on how God uses government to accomplish His will.

2. Write a short paper on a tax-saving idea that you researched on the Web.

3. Make a presentation on the advantages and disadvantages of taxes.

4. Critically review a tax system in a country other than the United States and present your findings.

PART THREE

Stewardship Planning and the Future

CHAPTER 9

Biblical Perspective on Insurance

Learning Objectives

1. Be able to show the biblical basis for the concept of insurance.

2. Describe the purpose and history of insurance and how it relates to the biblical concept of making another whole.

3. Describe the important forms of insurance that Christians should consider.

Lord, I commit to trusting in you.

Lord, I realize that you are the source of life and you know what the future holds for me and my family. As I set aside funds and plan for the unexpected I commit to trusting you for my needs. Help me by your Spirit to understand the role insurance plays in that plan and to wisely choose the avenues that would best protect the assets that you have and will provide to me. Help me not to rely on insurance as a means to take away my trust in you but recognize, as a good steward, that it is a financial tool to be carefully used.

Insurance - Making Things Whole

We now embark on a topic that can have a profound effect on your financial planning. That topic is insurance. There is much that is misunderstood about insurance and from the Christian's perspective the question of whether it is biblical to rely on insurance rather than God is often raised. In this section we explore the history and purpose of insurance as well as look at the Christian's perspective on insurance.

The Biblical Perspective

We should first note that the word insurance does not occur in the Bible. The definition we would be most familiar with is a contract by which one party agrees to indemnify or reimburse for a loss of another. Insurance comes from the Latin word for "security." That is, there is an assurance that if there is a loss it will be reimbursed. The question that will be raised by many Christians is whether acquiring insurance shows a lack of faith. Unfortunately, this question causes unnecessary duress for the believer. To raise the question as one of faith would lead us to question whether we need to work or invest since they could show a lack of faith as well. The reason we do invest and work without casting doubt on our faith in God is because we see in the scriptures the importance of doing these things as part of our faith. As we shall see this is the same for insurance.

Did you ever notice that our English word invest is not mentioned in the Bible? Yet based on the Scriptures it is very clear that we should invest properly. The same is true of insurance. The word insurance is not mentioned but we do see the principle of insurance at work. The objective of insurance is to indemnify or reimburse for a loss; that is, to provide a substitute for something lost; whether you do it yourself (self-insured) by not buying insurance, or whether you purchase that protection from another. By not having insurance you have implicitly agreed to reimburse others for any losses they sustain as a result of any error on your part. This is quite biblical. First take a look at Exodus 21:18-19. It states "if men dispute, and one strike the other with a stone, or with his fist, and he die not, but take to his bed, - if he rise, and walk abroad upon his staff, then shall he that struck him be guiltless; only he shall pay for the loss of his time, and shall cause him to be thoroughly healed" (JND). Did you ever notice this verse? It basically says that if you were the cause for another to lose time that you must make it up – completely – by paying for the lost time. Let's take a look further down in the same chapter. In verses 33-35 it states "if a man open a pit, or if a man dig a pit, and do not cover it, and an ox or an ass fall into it, the owner of the pit shall make it good, shall give money to the owner of them and the dead (ox or ass) shall be his" (JND). Again we see the principle at work. If we cause the loss for another then we are required to make that individual whole by repaying for the loss. Exodus 22 also

provides many other examples including if you provide safe-keeping of something for a neighbor (7 ff.) or borrow something and it becomes hurt or broken (14-15).

God makes clear in His Word that making another whole by a fault of yours is biblical. Our choices can lead to errors that hurt others and as a result we need to make them whole. Whether we do that implicitly (by being self-insured) or by the use of a financial instrument is also a choice we can make. The issue is not one of faith in God but recognizing that as humans we do err and we need to plan to reimburse those we cause to have losses. Acquiring insurance is just one way of providing for that situation. Others save some funds aside for that purpose. Others do not plan and as a result may go through grave difficulties and perhaps bankruptcy in order to make another whole they have wronged. Now, we should note here that insurance has gone beyond the initial goal of providing for the losses of others caused by you. We now have all types of insurance including life, long-term care, disability, natural disaster, and the like. These also reimburse for a loss but not for one necessarily caused by you. That is, many of these indemnify for actions of others or nature in its operations. These do not appear to cause any issue either as we must understand that events that have resulted in the creation of these forms of insurance do occur over time as part of the way the world operates. We can also see these same events in the Bible. The difference is in how the provision for the loss occurred in the past – usually through the support of the community. As we will discuss under the history of insurance, in the past insurance was acquired by becoming part of a community. In highly developed nations this in many ways has been at least partially replaced by insurance. We see, though, that areas where insurance is not prevalent the community still plays an important role as in the recovery from the tsunami that created a disaster in many nations in the Far East several years ago.

> "If we cause the loss for another then we are required to make that individual whole by repaying for the loss."

Based on our discussion here, then, Christians should at a minimum have no difficulty in acquiring insurance that provides for losses to others caused by their actions. This would include automobile insurance, home insurance (at least to some degree), liability insurance, and other insurances that cover actions of yours that may cause harm to others (such as boat insurance). Some of these policies, such as home insurance, also provide for you in case of the loss of the home. The only ones that Christians are usually required to purchase actually fall under the group we have mentioned – automobile and home (if you have a mortgage). If you live in a flood plain you may be required to purchase flood insurance if you have a mortgage. Of course the Christian is not required to live in a flood plain if they wish to avoid this type of insurance. Whether you wish to acquire other forms of insurance such as life, long-term care, and disability should be a decision between each family or individual and the Lord. If your heart is right with the Lord and you carefully use these as a part of being a good steward and not for the wrong purpose then these other forms of insurance would be fine for the Christian to consider. The final decision must be left between the individual and the Lord. If, as a matter of conscience, the believer will only purchase legally required insurance then there is no problem with that. Not every form of insurance is necessary and the good steward needs to be aware of which ones a steward should use and those to avoid.

The History of Insurance

Although it may be impossible to trace the history of insurance back to its origins it has been around for a long time. Earliest recorded instances of the idea go back to Babylon and its merchants who would pay a premium to the one who provided capital for his goods in return for the cancellation of the loan if the merchant were robbed of his goods. Before this type of arrangement the merchant would lose all he owned and he and his family would become slaves. Basically the banker took on the risk of the loan for the payment of some additional amount from the merchant.

Over the years there have been various societies and clubs that have been formed for the purpose of sharing in any losses. Especially when we get to the times of the Romans, the idea of sharing losses became very pronounced in the form of guilds and burial societies where the cost of burial was shared by the members of the society. In these early efforts of insurance, profit was not the motive but the sharing of any risk related to an event. This idea of the community sharing in the losses was also evident in the early days of America.

Insurance as we know it was instituted after the Great London Fire of 1666. It burned over 400 acres of the city destroying thousands of buildings. Nicholas Barbon who had witnessed the tragedy of the London fire was moved to open an office to insure buildings. He established the first fire insurance company, the Fire Office in 1680. Soon after that was the establishment of the first "mutual" insurance company in 1696. Its title, although long, does convey the idea of sharing. Its name was "Contributorship for Insuring Houses, Chambers, or Rooms from Loss by Fire by Amicable Contributions."

The key difference we see today from what insurance used to be is that insurance companies now play the role of pooling together funds to be shared. Of course,

they also take a portion for their work in making this a reality and taking on the risk associated with making members feel secure against a loss. As a result, we do not have near the level of community support and sharing we once had, although we do still see glimpses of it in major disasters or when a particular family has suffered a horrendous loss that moves people to action.

As this brief history then shows, insurance really is a shared way in dealing with reimbursement for loss. We would not be able to call this unbiblical since the idea of making one whole is biblical. If the intent of insurance is other than this then we have a biblical problem. Some have erred in trying to become rich off insurance by trying to find ways to collect on their policies even if no loss has actually occurred (feigning disability, staging accidents, etc.). When our heart seeks to go beyond the intention of the provision we have gone beyond where God would have us to go.

The Purpose of Insurance

Now that we have seen the biblical perspective and the brief history of insurance we see that its purpose is to provide for a loss. We have seen that losses caused by us are certainly something we should seek to provide for, while providing for other types of losses should be carefully weighed, as good stewards, trying to keep our Lord's assets intact and earning a return. Since the purpose of insurance is to provide in the event of a loss, it

becomes clear that whatever insurance we do acquire we should hope that we never have to use it. That is, it is one expense that you pay into a pool that you hope you never get a return on. In order to get a return on insurance you must suffer a loss. So the lesson here is do not purchase insurance for any reason other than to plan for a possible loss. God can provide through the use of insurance when considered as an appropriate part of the financial planning portfolio and used in the proper way.

Although there is one purpose for insurance, the world has sought to abuse the opportunity provided by insurance by adding other features or using it as a replacement for careful stewardship. This is why many Christians have difficulty with insurance. They see the world's view of let's insure anything and everything so we can feel secure. The Christian recognizes that he is secure in Christ and that regardless of events or level of insurance that security in Christ remains. The problem is not insurance itself but when we remove our trust from Christ and put it in ourselves. By at least planning for losses or insurance we recognize that neither we nor the world is perfect. By not planning we make the assumption that nothing will go wrong (the world is perfect) or we think that God will fix whatever goes wrong. Some call this having faith in God but this thinking usually signifies a misunderstanding of how God operates in the world. The Bible and experience shows that although God can, and will at times intervene in the events of the world, He also allows men to make poor decisions and nature to run its course. The wise steward prepares for the events that emanate from these before they occur.

One example we can review is that of Joseph in Egypt (Genesis 41). He learned from God that there would be a famine. God foreknew the event and just made Joseph aware of the fact that was what nature would bring to bear. Now keep in mind that God did not show Joseph anything about what to do about the famine in the dream (at least we are not told He did). Joseph could have told the Pharaoh about the dream and let it go at that and figure that God would take care of it from there. Rather, Joseph, likely after careful prayer, devised a plan to neutralize the natural event by storing up grain as security against the famine. Yet, certainly Joseph was trusting in God. Again, the issue is one of the heart. We want to encourage you to seek God's guidance on what insurance is appropriate as part of the larger plan of being a good steward of what God has provided. We do not want to lose all of what He has provided to an event that we could have planned for.

Insurance – Your Plan

Your Plan for Insurance

After reading the previous sections on insurance, you may be convinced of its appropriateness as a part of the personal financial planning process as a Christian. Your next question might be – what kinds are appropriate as part of the plan? In this section we will note the key insurance vehicles to consider

Automobile Insurance. It probably goes without saying that people make mistakes when driving and cause losses of their own as well as to others. Biblically as we have seen, we are enjoined to at least make the others that we affect whole. Also, most states require some kind of automobile insurance to drive a vehicle. The recommendation then is to purchase appropriate automobile insurance for your vehicle or vehicles.

Home/Renter's Insurance. Home insurance not only provides coverage for you if you should lose your home to a natural event but it also helps you make others whole who might suffer a loss on your property. If someone injures himself on your property then it is normally expected that you will pay the appropriate medical expenses and perhaps lost time out of work. Again, purchasing this type of policy is appropriate to cover others at a minimum. You may also be required to carry certain coverage for your home if there is a mortgage on the home. If you have no mortgage you will need to decide whether you can afford to pay any claims against you or rebuild your home if something does happen on your property. If you are a renter you will need to decide whether you can cover the loss of all your personal belongings or for another who is hurt through your fault in your apartment or home. Your personal property is not normally covered by the owner's policy if you are renting.

Health Insurance. This one is more difficult in several ways. First, the goal is not to make another whole but to provide for yourself or a family member. Second, no matter how you look at it healthcare is expensive. For a family with children today having healthcare coverage is worth pursuing in order to protect the family's other assets. The goal should be to reduce the insurance costs as much as possible by keeping a savings account for a large deductible. Premiums are much lower for health insurance if the company knows that it will not be paying for every visit to the doctor's office. Here your goal is to protect your assets against a major claim from a major health disease or accident. An operation today can cost many thousands of dollars and quickly wipe out an emergency fund or other assets.

Life Insurance. As with health insurance the goal of this form of insurance is to protect those in your family. Here, the protection is also in a sense related to assets since the goal of life insurance is to provide funds for those living if the one who earns money for the family dies. If there is no life insurance then the family must live off of the assets that are left. Whether to acquire life insurance should again be a personal decision based on your situation. If purchased, it should be for those who earn the income since the intent is to provide for a loss of income. Though one occasionally benefits, life insurance policies on children make no sense since they are not earning an income and their life expectancy is quite long. In addition, the policies are ridiculously expensive. Life insurance makes sense for a young family until they have built their assets enough where they could survive the loss of the income of the earning family member. As you get older your need for life insurance should decrease as your assets grow and your expenses go down with children out of the home and on their own.

Disability Insurance. Research shows that many do become disabled at some point in their lives, even if it is for a brief time. Again, this form of insurance is to protect the family's income when the wage earner cannot work. Since this is not to protect others outside the family the decision is up to the family or individual whether to pursue this form of insurance. It is best to try to get this kind of insurance through your employer. Otherwise, the policies are quite expensive. We would recommend having insurance in this area as a way of protecting assets if a disability were to occur but again this should be a matter of conscience.

Liability Insurance. Your home and automobile policies likely have some form of liability insurance that pays another when you are at fault. The goal of additional liability insurance is to protect assets that you would be required to use if you were served with a judgment where you were at fault. Those with significant assets should consider acquiring an "umbrella policy" that covers most types of liability especially since it helps to make another whole that you have harmed.

Long-Term Care Insurance. Over the last 25 years long-term care insurance has become very popular. This is because people are living longer and the cost of healthcare as people age is increasing. As people age they are also more likely to end up in an assisted living facility or nursing home. These are very expensive places to live. This, again, is something the individual or family must carefully consider. If it is possible for the loved one to remain at home and receive care from outside the home such as hospice care, then that could be an inexpensive option. There is no easy answer to this one since each family is different and has a different number of members to help support it.

There are many other forms of insurance, but these are the only ones a Christian needs to seriously consider. Many others are just money-making ventures for the companies who purvey them with little value to the policy holder. This does not mean that one may not find a

need for another form such rental car insurance or travel insurance. Generally though there are other avenues for eliminating these expensive forms of insurance.

Reducing Premiums. A key component of your plan, in addition to having adequate coverage in the area of insurance, is to keep the amount of premiums you pay to a minimum. The more you save on premiums the more that is available for investing and building your assets – which of course can lead to further reductions in premiums. There are many factors that can influence premiums and will be somewhat different depending on the type of insurance. Generally, the more risk (and willingness to pay) you take the lower the premiums.

You should also keep in mind, as a general point, that credit scores are now often used in determining premiums, especially in the areas of auto and home insurance. A correlation has been identified that those who are poor credit risks also file more claims for insurance. It's a good idea to check your credit report and make sure it is right. If you have had problems in the credit area start now to build good credit so your premiums can go down in the future.

Christian Support

Before closing this chapter we need to note that some of the needs for insurance can be offset by Christians' willingness to support each other. Before the modern era families would care for one another in their homes or support the widows and infirmed. Today, as we have noted, the community aspect has been for the most part replaced by companies that provide the sharing of the funds through insurance. For the church, though, there are many examples, especially in the New Testament, that show how the saints cared for and supported one another. We would like to encourage those who have the means to be a support for those who are widows indeed, or for those who are infirmed or disabled. Some of the costs of insurance could be reduced by Christians working together to support one another.

Share Plans. Some Christians have made efforts to get back to the original community sharing aspect of Christians helping one another in the body of Christ. For instance, Medi-Share is one group where members support one another's healthcare costs. They can be reached at www.biblicalhealthcare.com. Another is Samaritan Ministries at www.samaritanministries.org which uses a similar model but is different in how it collects and distributes the funds. We know of several people that have been pleased with this group. These are not considered insurance but considered medical cost sharing. Like insurance there is a monthly "share" that you pay based on the coverage you desire. There are also amounts you must pay first before being allowed to share in the pooled monthly shares. These are similar to the insurance "deductibles." The real plus of this type of approach is that members of the share group are expected to live according to biblical principles, which encourage a healthy, less risky lifestyle. This type of plan may be worth investigating but be sure you understand all the requirements and rules before you sign up. These groups may also have an application and annual renewal fee for some of its plans.

Exercises and Research Activities

1. Research an example from the Bible that shows that we are responsible to right any wrong that we have committed. Write a brief summary and be prepared to share your thoughts.

2. By reading or interviewing others, find out why individuals buy insurance. Write up a report on your findings and be sure to include a comparison to the biblical perspective.

3. Create an insurance plan for you, and if you have one, your family. Include the types of insurance and the amounts of coverage you believe you need. Identify why you chose the amount of coverage you did for each.

Biblical Perspective on Investing

Lord, I commit to providing a return.

Lord, thank you for the financial resources you have provided to me while walking here below. I desire to use them for your glory and to provide you an abundant return. I commit to you now to use these resources in such a way that they will create a return that is pleasing to you. Give me wisdom as I seek to establish accounts that will be appropriate for the use of the resources you provide. Thank you for your continued strength as I learn more about investing for your glory.

The Biblical Perspective on Investing

Investing deals with putting assets to use for a return in the future. There is no doubt that the Bible provides a multitude of examples of those who are wise, investing for the future. The perspective is both material and spiritual. That is, the Bible speaks of the importance of laying up for ourselves treasures in heaven as well as being a good steward on earth. The point of this is that the world has no way of taking those treasures that are in heaven. The Bible also speaks of being a good steward, investing in the present so there will be plenty in the future. Joseph is an example of this in Genesis 41 where he, by God's will, saw the coming famine and stored up food in a time of plenty so there would be food available during the famine. One might question this example as an investment. Where is the return? The return was in the saved lives in Egypt as well as the price they received for the grain during the famine. The return was not immediate but it indeed was great.

The Spiritual Perspective — For the Master

The first point to be understood concerning investing for the future is that it must be of God and for Him and His glory. Many are the sad stories of well-intentioned Christians rushing into the "can't miss" opportunities only to find too late they have little or nothing left for their investment. Worse still, is that many Christians will focus on developing a financial portfolio with little thought to the heavenly one.

Let us note, then, that any investing must be done for the Master (laying up treasure in heaven) and not for ourselves. That is, we recognize that God allows us to invest what He has provided that He might provide for others and ourselves in the future. The key is that any return belongs to Him as well. It is when we recognize that the "treasure" and the return are His that we can be free in responsibly investing it.

We must also recognize that laying up spiritual treasure also involves investing in spiritual things. These include studying His Word, praying, and serving Him. Spiritual returns can only occur if these are also part of the "investment mix." Matthew 6:19-21 serves as a good reminder of this where it speaks of "treasures in heaven." The Bible reminds us on more than one occasion that our citizenship is not earthly but heavenly. Ephesians 2:19 emphasizes that the household of Christians is now of God and not the world. It states "so then ye are no more strangers and foreigners, but ye are fellow-citizens of the saints, and of the household of God" (JND). Philippians 3:20 reminds us that "our commonwealth has its existence in the heavens, from which also we await the Lord Jesus Christ as Savior (JND). If we expect to have a spiritual return we must be investing in spiritual things.

Remember that both literal and spiritual investing are for the Master, our Lord Jesus Christ.

The Spiritual Perspective — If God Will

The second key area in understanding the biblical perspective of investing is to recognize that all must be done according to His will. You may ask; how do we know His will? Well, this goes back to our first point - investing time in His Word and prayer. God has already made known to us His will through the Word. The difficulty lies in putting aside the enticements of the world to pursue what God has to say. For young people this can be extremely difficult because there are so many things clamoring for their time and attention. You cannot know the Lord's will in your life if you do not know Him, are not reading what He has said, and asking Him for guidance.

Seeking the Master's will is a great way to keep the "flesh" in check. Remember the "flesh" or old nature lusts after the things of the world and so physical riches can be very enticing. Paul notes in 1 Timothy 6:9 that "those who desire to be rich fall into temptation and a snare, and many unwise and hurtful lusts, which plunge men into destruction and ruin" (JND). In this verse we see the lust of the flesh at work that can ruin a man and his testimony. This becomes clear in verse 10 where it notes that some that have coveted after money have "wandered from the faith, and pierced themselves through with many sorrows" (JND).

See, anything financial including investing must be according to His will and Word. As to making an investment gain James makes it very clear that it should be undertaken with – "if the Lord will." James 4:13-15 states "go to now, ye who say, today or tomorrow will we go into such a city and spend a year there and traffic and make gain, ye who do not know what will be on the morrow, (for what is your life? It is even a vapor, appearing for a little while, and then disappearing,) instead of your saying, if the Lord should so will and we should live, we will also do this or that" (JND). This makes it clear that the Bible has no problem with investing or trading and making gain. The question becomes is your heart right and are you taking steps - if the Lord should so will? Working outside of His will is bound to lead to much sorrow in the future.

Perhaps you have heard the saying "there is no free lunch".

The Spiritual Perspective — Effort is Required

Perhaps you have heard the saying "there is no free lunch." Now, perhaps you have had an occasional free lunch from someone but the adage goes beyond the physical lunch. Have you ever received an email from Nigeria saying that you can have millions of dollars or a chain letter that asks you to send 20 dollars to five different people so you will get many thousands? These requests at times seem very real but whenever something sounds too good to be true, it likely is. The Nigerian email still makes its rounds and after the initial round some "investors" lost $20 million. These types of scams or "investments" prey on the flesh's desires and are basically a "get rich quick" scenario that entices the flesh within. The point here is that investing requires an effort over time. Get rich quick scenarios usually try to mitigate these factors by noting there is little for you to do and you can be enriched in a very short period of time. This is against the very nature of storing up or investing.

In Matthew 25:14-30 the Lord uses an investment related parable to describe the kingdom of heaven Not only does the parable teach us a spiritual lesson about using what God gives by the Spirit during this present age for a return for His glory but gives us a general lesson about investing our earthly goods for the Master's glory as well. There are several things to note about this parable. First God gives according to as a man is able. There is a choice on God's part of how much He will entrust to your care. Second, there is time (the Master is now in heaven until he comes for us) and effort involved (they went and traded). Third, as you are faithful in what has been given to you additional resources and responsibilities will then be given to you. It is important to note that we cannot feign being a servant of His. Many are those today who profess to know Christ and give the semblance of serving Him but are unprofitable. This was the case of the wicked servant in this parable. If he were a true servant he would have at least put the Master's money in the bank to receive interest. The true servant always has a return for the Master. In Matthew 7:22 the Lord notes that many will say "Lord, Lord, have we not prophesied through thy name…" and the Lord in the following verse says, "I never knew you" (JND). Be sure your motives in investing are right and in line with what the Lord would have. Do not use Him as a cover for trying to get physically rich in this present world as many do today who preach the "health and wealth gospel."

The Spiritual Perspective — Plan Before Action

There are numerous scriptures that deal with faithfulness in the use of our resources and emphasize the point we have been making. In addition, they point to the importance of planning before taking action. Proverbs 28:20 notes "a faithful man shall abound with blessing, but he that maketh haste to be rich shall not be innocent" (KJV). That is, the one who hastens to be rich will not go unpunished. Although there appears to be blessing the result in the end is not. The Bible is clear here that

we are not to pursue the "get rich quick" schemes of the world. We have already noted several including chain letters, but this would also include lotteries, gambling, and uneducated, high-risk investing such as options, derivatives, and the like. The goal of all these is generally, to get rich quickly. Almost invariably you lose in these situations either literally and/or spiritually. The godly woman of Proverbs 31 is an example of one who is careful and diligent in the use of her resources to build for her family's future. Verse 16 notes that she "considereth a field, and buyeth it; with the fruit of her hands she planteth a vineyard" (v. 16, KJV). She is careful to use her mind to consider what she should do and actually invests several different ways. She plans before she acts. Proverbs 21:5 reminds us that "the thoughts of the diligent tend only to plenteousness, but of everyone that is hasty only to want" (KJV). So too, we need to plan and consider what God would have us to do before we act in the area of investing as with the other areas of finance. Other verses to consider in relation to this include Proverbs 23:4-5, 24:3-4, 27:1, and 28:22.

Prerequisites to Investing

Before you look at various investment instruments note some key characteristics that should be evident in the Christian who would desire to invest. These would include:

Establishing Discipline in Giving. The Lord desires that we give, so part of demonstrating discipline is giving back to God, on a regular basis, a portion of that He has given to us. Many characteristics of the good investor are the same as those of a good biblical giver.

Operating on a Spending Plan or Budget. As we have learned those who do not plan carefully will have difficulty in being successful in any aspect of financial stewardship. Diligence in following a budget is a good indicator of whether one will have the diligence necessary to research and invest wisely.

Spending Less Than You Earn. You will not have anything to invest unless you spend less than your income.

Living Within Your Means. Similar to the previous characteristic this characteristic emphasizes careful thinking and planning for larger purchases rather than overspending to have everything now. Good investors need to look for a return over the long term.

Establishing an Emergency Fund. As we have noted before, unless an emergency fund has been established the budget will encounter regular attacks which will make it very difficult to be effective in saving regularly. Building up a fund also shows the ability to save regularly for investment.

Eliminating High-Interest Debt. Investment returns will likely be much lower than high-interest credit card or other unsecured debt. Paying down high-interest debt is almost always a better investment.

Save for Major Purchases. As we have noted it is best to save for major purchases. The ability to save for major purchases is a good indication of one who can also invest regularly. It also eliminates the need to spend money on interest on a loan for a major purchase.

Exercises and Research Activities

1. Choose a Bible passage that appears to deal with investing and explain the lessons it shows us.

2. Write a brief report on what characteristics should be evident in an individual's life before he or she begins investing and why are they important.

3. Research an article that deals with some of the investing issues and write a brief annotation that outlines what you learned.

Christian Life Planning

Lord, I commit to being used of you in retirement.

Lord, I know I may be young now but at some point, if you so will, I will be older and my body will get to a point that it will be ready to retire from the physical labors it once could endure. I commit now, though, to not languish in retirement or just take my ease, but to be used of you as you would see fit. Help me to build assets so that I might be a help to my family and to your work when it becomes time to retire. Please let your Spirit guide me now and in the future as I seek to glorify you in this life whether young or old.

Life Planning –
The Retirement Years

Many of you reading this book may be college age and thinking that retirement is so far away that it is something that can wait for a later time. As we noted earlier, the time value of money has a profound effect on your future assets and what you will have available to support you, your family, and the Lord's work. By ignoring the issue while young you will lose out on the opportunity to better provide in the future. These next two chapters, then, are included to encourage you to take a more significant look at this area while you are young so that you may be an instrument of the Lord when you are older. The fact that people are living longer should also give us pause to consider how we will support those extra years of retirement and yet still be of service to Him.

The Biblical Perspective on Age

The Lord's measurement of time is quite different from ours as 2 Peter 3:8 makes clear: "one day with the Lord is as a thousand years and a thousand years as one day" (JND). In reality though our time on earth may seem long to us but in God's eyes it is but a few hours. Thankfully, for us, the Bible has been written to take into account our understanding of time. In fact, there seems to be a general positive perspective on old age noted in the Scripture. Of course in today's society to use the term "old age" would not be viewed as politically correct. Perhaps "mature adults" is now the phrase of the hour. In any case the Bible does not see the phrase "old age" as a negative.

We would do well to understand that "old age" is seen as a positive in the Bible. Genesis 25:8 notes that Abraham lived 175 years and that he "died in a good old age, old and full of days" (JND). That God looks at old age as an honor is clear by the instructions He gave to Moses for Israel. In Leviticus 19:32 he notes that "before the hoary head thou shalt rise up, and shalt honour the face of an old man and thou shalt fear thy God: I am Jehovah" (JND). We wonder if this is how we view those who are older – ones to whom honor is due for their maturity. Evidently, not to have an old man in the house was not seen as a good thing. 1 Samuel 2:31-32 records Eli being told that because of his sons' sin that "there shall not be an old man in thy house…there shall not be an old man in thy house forever" (JND).

There is no question of course that at times age also brings a reduction in the body's ability to maintain itself against disease. Eli, just as is common today as people advance in age, could not see as he was dim in the eyes (1 Samuel 3:2). That those who are older can be of help due to their experience and many years of walking with the Lord is clear. Rehoboam sought the counsel of the old men but forsook their counsel to his detriment (1

Kings 12:6-8). We do not have the space to go through the entire Bible and look at each verse related to those who are old but it becomes clear as you read, that for the Israelites a long life was a blessing from God to those who followed Him. In the same vein Christians are blessed with a lasting spiritual life if they continue to follow Christ. Our physical life may not be assured as being long but our spiritual life is if we follow Him for that life will continue into eternity.

In summary, then, old age is normally seen as a good thing and a time when one can still be used of God in helping others along the right path as counselors who have had many years of experience to draw on. Though the physical body may tire, the believer's spiritual life can continue to flourish and can still be used of God for His service.

The Biblical Perspective on Retirement

Seeing, then, that older age is a good thing, it is important to understand what God has to say about what we do during that time. In our society we call that time retirement. For many, this has the unfortunate connotation of taking our ease and traveling with little regard of being of service to God and others. The biblical mandate is quite different. Although there is the indication that our physical labors to support us may be reduced or cease, our other labors of love in the Lord should not. The one time that "retire" is noted in the Bible, as we know the term, is in Numbers 8:24-26. It is a great lesson for what retirement is about. It says "Jehovah spoke to Moses, saying, This is that which concerneth the Levites: from twenty-five years old, and upward shall he come to labour in the work of the service of the tent of meeting. And from fifty years old he shall retire from the labour of the service, and shall serve no more; but he shall minister with his brethren in the tent of meeting, and keep the charge, but he shall not serve in the service" (JND).

"One day with the Lord is as a thousand years and a thousand years as one day." 2 Pet. 3:8

There does come a time when the "labor" ceases as we know it but the "ministering" continues. The biblical perspective is never seen as one of taking your ease but rather reducing the labor that is difficult for the body and increasing the opportunity to minister in the things of the Lord. That we should bring forth fruit for the Lord during retirement permeates the Bible. Psalms 92:13-15 states "those that are planted in the house of Jehovah shall flourish in the courts of our God. They are still vigorous in old age, they are full of sap and green; to shew that Jehovah is upright: he is my rock, and there is no unrighteousness in him" (JND). Proverbs

20:29 notes that the beauty of old men is their grey head. That is, in symbol the grey hair identifies one who has a mature understanding from years of being in the presence of God.

The New Testament continues on the same theme concerning the aged. In fact, the church, as described in its functioning, is headed up by a plurality of "elders" rather than by a pastor as many know it today. That is, it was men who were mature in the Lord and had devoted themselves to the Word and demonstrated by their life and their handling of their family that they were capable as men over God's house. Paul in his letter to Titus also recognizes that the aged men and women play a continued role in God's work even if they may not work for their sustenance. He notes "that the elder men be sober, grave, discreet, sound in faith, in love, in patience; that the elder women in like manner be in deportment as becoming those who have the say to sacred things, not slanderers, not enslaved to much wine, teachers of what is right, that they may admonish the young women..." (Titus 2:2-4 JND).

It becomes clear that as we prepare for retirement that we must be prayerfully considering what that retirement will involve. The idea that retirement will just be a time to relax and watch television is foreign to Scripture. Scripture sees older men and women still as able ministers for the Lord. The beauty of retirement is that it allows you more time to help others in the Lord's name or to minister with your spiritual gifts more frequently than when you had to work full-time. So although retirement can provide some rest for the body as it ages, it does not preclude the steward from continuing to minister for the Lord. You can be used greatly of the Lord in your retirement if you plan ahead.

The Financial Plan

As you would do as a steward before retirement you should also do as a steward after retirement. Just because you enter retirement does not mean you no longer have to be a good steward. At times people look at retirement as an opportunity to spend all that they have saved but this certainly does not follow the biblical perspective of being a good steward and providing for His work.

If we are going to be good stewards in retirement then we must have a financial plan as we would if we were not retiring. Of key importance, for those retiring, is that their income may be more limited than before retirement. As a result, they will need to be sure that their expenses are budgeted so that they are in line with the income expected. Retirees should use the same methodology in retirement as they would when younger when developing a financial spending plan. If you have been careful with your expenses as you have matured then it is likely that most if not all your costs related to children are past and

you have hopefully paid off any debt related to your home and credit cards.

As you plan and budget keep in mind that there will likely be increases in spending for healthcare as you get older and your insurance premiums may rise for health and auto related insurance policies. If you own a home then you may be able to reduce your taxes as some communities have reductions for senior citizens.

Exhibit 11-1 provides a checklist of items to review in preparation for your retirement years. Be sure you have reviewed all of the appropriate documents and know how things will be covered and be taken care of if you should become unable to take care of your finances on your own. Good planning using this checklist can save your family from much consternation when having to deal with unexpected difficulties you might have. Most financial planning books will cover details of these documents.

Retirement Documentation Checklist	
Retirement Spending Plan	☐
Estate and Inheritance Plan	☐
Medical Directives/Living Will	☐
Power of Attorney	☐
Trusts if Appropriate	☐
Last Will and Testament	☐
Funeral Instructions	☐

Exhibit 11-1. Retirement Documentation Checklist.

The key here is planning ahead based on the possible scenarios. It is always easier to plan in case of something occurring rather than trying to come up with a solution when something does occur. Proverbs 21:5 notes that "the plans of the diligent lead surely to advantage" (KJV).

Reverse Mortgages

It might be good to cover another topic that often comes up in relation to senior housing or providing income for seniors and that is the subject of reverse mortgages. Many of the aged own homes but financially cannot take care of all their expenses. That is, much of the net worth is wrapped up in the illiquid form of the home. This has resulted in the creation of a mortgage product that lets those who have reached a certain age and own their home to tap into the equity it contains by receiving a monthly payment from the bank. This product is called a reverse mortgage.

With a reverse mortgage the amount of the loan on a home increases each month as a payment is made by the bank to the owner of the home. Interest is charged on the amount of the loan currently outstanding which, of course, will also grow as the loan grows and the interest is compounded. The loan is paid off on the sale of the home with the remainder of the proceeds going to the owner or his beneficiaries. The owner must keep up with taxes and repairs so the home is not foreclosed on. If the amount owed exceeds the value of the home the lender takes the loss.

The two key benefits for the aged are the increased income from tapping the equity in their home and the ability to continue to live in their home. The advantages though come at a significant cost. Upfront fees and non-interest fees can take up to 10 percent of the value of the home. This could include 5 percent for mortgage insurance premiums, 2 percent for servicing fees, 2 percent for origination fees for the loan, and 1 percent for closing costs. With all these costs it does not make sense to get a reverse mortgage if you will be moving soon. The interest rates are often adjustable. Another minus is that depending on the type of reverse mortgage, if the owner needs to sell the home sooner than he planned, he will need to pay off the loan. He will also have less of an inheritance to pass on or a home that has been in the family for many years may no longer stay in the family.

There should be no surprise that even reverse mortgages can be used as a way to feed another's greed since some prey on seniors who might be more trusting. Some unscrupulous companies and individuals have used high-pressure tactics to get seniors to take out a reverse mortgage and then use the proceeds to buy annuities or insurance policies from them that have significant fees or penalties. Be careful as there are many reverse mortgage scams. A reverse mortgage can be helpful but should only be considered as one of the final remedies to financial difficulties.

Exercises and Research Activities

1. Write a brief abstract on what your hopes for the future are and what you expect to do during retirement if the Lord tarries.

2. Think carefully about the future and try to come up with an idea of how much you will need to live on each year during retirement. Assume you live 25 years during retirement. How much would you need at the beginning of retirement to have enough to get you through it assuming a 7% return on your assets?

Will We Have Been Found Faithful?

Lord, I commit to being a faithful steward.

Lord, as I come to end of my life here on earth I hope that you will have found me faithful to you as a good steward of what you have provided. I hope that the legacy I leave to those in this world will be one that speaks loudly of your sustaining grace and provision in my life. I give you the honor and glory for all that you have done and intend to do in my life. I find it hard to express in words what you mean to me so I will simply say "thank you" for your love to me.

Estate Planning – Inheritance

We now come to our final chapter of study together and it is fitting that it deals with the final chapter in our earthly lives of dealing with the future of our estate that is left once the life in our physical bodies dies. Although at this point you may be quite young and feel that such things are a long way off, experience shows that no one knows ahead of time when the precise time will be that death occurs. So it is important as a good steward to prepare in advance for this certainty of life. This chapter will help you to prepare for that time.

The Biblical Perspective on Wills and Inheritance

As we have done throughout the text, as we have embarked on various personal financial planning topics, we have made an effort to study what the Word of God has to say about a particular matter. As with most financially-related topics the Word is not silent concerning the issues of estates and inheritance.

We should first note that as Christians we have a spiritual inheritance that the world cannot know. Our hope is an inheritance in the heavenlies and not on the earth. The Jews, of course, looked for a physical inheritance such as the land in Canaan flowing with milk and honey and were to keep that inheritance in the family (Numbers 36:7-9). It is interesting to note, though, that the Levites received no inheritance in the land. They were priests to God and God was their inheritance. It says that "to the tribe of Levi, Moses did not give an inheritance; the Lord, the God of Israel, is their inheritance, as He had promised them" (Joshua 13:33, KJV). The Levites, of course, are symbolic of the Christians who are also priests as 1 Peter 2:5 makes clear: "yourselves also, as living stones, are being built up a spiritual house, a holy priesthood, to offer spiritual sacrifices acceptable to God by Jesus Christ" (JND). Today as Christians, we are more concerned with our spiritual inheritance, or at least we should be. Paul in Galatians notes "but because ye are sons, God has sent out the Spirit of His Son into our hearts, crying Abba, Father. So thou art no longer bondman, but son; but if son; heir also through God (4:6-7, JND).

Beyond the spiritual inheritance that we look forward to, we will leave earthly property or an estate when we die. If we look at the issue of estates, most recognize that once death occurs the future disposition of the estate is most likely controlled by a will or other similar document such as a trust. Some may be surprised to know that the importance of estates and wills is noted in the Bible. The parable of the prodigal son brings out how the estate is divided among the living heirs after the death of the father. In the culture of the prodigal son, a son evidently could request his inheritance in advance. Both sons in the parable received their inheritance early and one went as the parable states "and squandered his estate" or literally "dissipated his property" (Luke 15:13, JND). Now this parable has many lessons that we do not have the time to get into here, but it becomes clear that one's estate or property does have a future beyond his death. Do you know what it is?

In Hebrews 9:15-18 we see how the Greek word for "disposition" is either translated "covenant" or "testament." The context usually will provide the appropriate translation. In verses 16-17 it states "for where there is a testament, the death of the testator must needs come in. For a testament is of force, when men are dead, since it is in no way of force while the testator is alive" (JND). Rather than debate whether "covenant" is the better term here it becomes clear that the writer understood the concept of wills and that the provision for an estate after the death of the testator is important. Thus God, through His Son, has provided an inheritance to all those that are called sons. To make that inheritance available required the death of Christ. In addition, under this testament God has given time to allow others to become sons by accepting that the mediator's death was on their behalf. Once that time noted in the testament for becoming sons has ended, the inheritance is lost to those who have not become sons.

In this section on Hebrews we see a picture of how a will or testament works. The steward recognizes that the future of his estate must be provided for so that the inheritance goes to the appropriate place. For God, he has decided that it will only go to those who have become His children through Christ. What will it be for our estates? Will we be pleased to see how the remainder of our earthly estate is used? You can use it for His glory and the future support of your family if you plan ahead.

The Will

One of the most important documents related to the planning of your future estate is your will. Keep in mind, that no matter how little or how much you have for earthly possessions when you die it is still considered your "estate." We often think that "estate planning" is for those who have big homes with lots of land or have a great deal of earthly wealth. In reality whether you're rich or poor your possessions are considered your "estate." The "disposition" of your estate can be guided by you if you plan ahead by using a will. There are other ways of planning the future of your estate such as with the use of trusts. These are also legal documents that allow you as a grantor to grant your possessions to a trustee to manage for the benefit of your beneficiaries.

> "One of the most important documents related to the planning of your future estate is your will."

The will is a legal document prepared by you before your death that describes how your estate is to be distributed after your death. If you do not leave a will (sometimes called a last will and testament) then your estate will be considered intestate. That is, you have an estate for which you did not leave a testament for. Every state has laws on how an estate is to be distributed on the death of the estate owner. The difficulty is that the state's laws or court determinations on the distribution of your estate may not be as you would have planned. For instance, states care little about providing some of your estate for the benefit of the Lord's work even if that is what you would have desired. It is better to plan ahead and draw up a will. This can initially be done using samples available online or through a software package such as Quicken WillMaker Plus, which is created in partnership with Nolo (www.nolo.com). Nolo provides legal support books and information on most legal topics so that individuals can understand what to do in various legal situations. Its site is quite good for legal information and its books are quite good as well. You should use the services of a lawyer to review your will or other legal documents to be sure that they are correct for the state you live in and that they are properly signed and witnessed. You could, of course, have the lawyer create the will based on your desires but the more you can do up front the less expensive it will be to use the lawyer.

Whatever you put in your last will and testament will be become available for public review as part of the probate court documents. Probate is the process that a will goes through in the court in order to distribute the estate according to your wishes. So be careful what you put into the document since you never know how what you say might be used at some point in the future. Wills in most states must be typed and the individual making the will must be of sound mind and not under undue influence of others in creating it. Wills must be signed and witnessed by others who are not beneficiaries of the will.

"A good man leaves an inheritance to his children's children." Prov. 13:22

The Inheritance

In this section we want to briefly review the purpose of an inheritance and what it is composed of. Proverbs 13:22 notes that "a good man leaves an inheritance to his children's children" (KJV). We often think of an inheritance as money and certainly that is part of it but we should also recognize that we leave an inheritance by the life we live as well. Children pick up on the legacy that you live. If you have a life honoring to Christ then it is likely that will be modeled by your children and then by your children's children.

You want to be seen as a faithful steward of all that God has given to you including the distribution of your earthly goods that remain after you die. A good inheritance (not necessarily a large one) demonstrates your faithfulness as a steward. The purpose of the inheritance is to provide for the future of your family as can be seen by the Proverbs 13:22 verse as well as provide for the future of the Lord's work. Ecclesiastes 2:21 states that "there is a man whose labor is in wisdom and in knowledge, and in equity; yet to a man that hath not labored therein shall he leave it for his portion. This also is vanity and a great evil" (KJV). Solomon's concern was that whatever he left after he died would go to one who did not labor the same way he did in wisdom and knowledge. Thankfully we, through the mechanisms we have briefly noted, can be sure that our estate is left to those who are of the same mind as we in the labor that glorifies the Lord.

The Bible has much to say about inheritance both physically and spiritually but in both cases the object is to provide for those we love in our physical family as well as those in our spiritual family. Plan now that the inheritance that you leave will produce fruit for the Lord for many years to come.

Does What is Left Point to Faithfulness?

In this final subsection we briefly note a question to ask yourself, does what you will have left behind point to faithfulness? That is, when you die and those you leave on this earth start to go through all that you were steward of, will they see through it all one who was the faithful steward? Consider the foolish man who rather than planning for his future estate thought he would take his ease. Luke 12 gives the parable and part of it says "I will lay up all my produce and my good things; and I will say to my soul, Soul; thou hast much good things laid by for many years; repose thyself, eat, drink, and be merry. But God said to him, Fool, this night thy soul shall be required of thee and whose shall be what thou hast prepared" (18-20, JND). Clearly the fool was not being faithful. Yes, he had stored up much, but his heart was not right and his plan for its use was not as God would have. Developing a plan to use it for God's glory rather than frittering it away would have demonstrated a heart right with God and a faithful one at that.

Perhaps you have heard the song sung so well by Steve Green that is entitled "Find Us Faithful." The words and music are by John Mohr and speaks of the faithfulness in the race of life as described in 2 Timothy 4:7-9. Within that song we really get the message loud and clear that others can see our faithfulness in how we live our lives and in what we leave behind. It conveys that we are pilgrims on the narrow road in this world. Many others have gone before us with lives that are a testimony to God and examples to us. As a result, we run the race before us with a desire to leave evidence of God's faithfulness in our lives that others may be able to follow in our footsteps. When we part this earth it is hoped that what we leave behind is a testimony to God's sustaining grace and faithfulness that will lead many to seek Him. May, as the song notes, all that come behind us truly find us faithful.

Remember 1 Corinthians 4:2 – "it is sought in stewards that a man be found faithful" (JND). Our hope is that whether by death or by His coming for you in the air, that you can stand before Him as one who has been faithful. It is our hope that in some small measure this book has been used of the Lord in your life to help you to become a more faithful person to Him. May He receive the glory for any benefit that you derive from these pages "for of Him and through Him and for Him are all things: to Him be glory forever, Amen" (Romans 11:36, JND).

Exercises and Research Activities

1. Research wills and try to write up a sample one. If you have access to will making software try using that. What things do you think are important for your will?

2. Create a portfolio that contains all of the estate planning documents that are on your estate checklist. Be sure to include funeral instructions and any other personal instructions that are important to you.

3. Consider how you would want the remainder of your estate distributed when you die. Would your ideas change based on your age? If, so how?

4. Write a brief report on what you believe it means to be a faithful steward and identify ways you believe that you can be more like the model you should be.

APPENDIX A

Web Resource List

Index

Web Resource List

Calculators

BabyCenter.com. www.babycenter.com/tools.htm
Bankrate.com. www.bankrate.com/calculators.aspx
Bloomberg Calculators. www.bloomberg.com/invest/calculators/index.html
Choose to Save. www.choosetosave.org/calculators/
Cost of Living. www.erieri.com
Finance Center.
    www.financecenter.com/products/calculators
Financial Aid Calculators. www.finaid.org/calculators/
Financial Calculators. www.financialcalculators.com/
Kiplinger Tools. www.kiplinger.com/tools/
Lead Fusion. www.leadfusion.com
Money-zine Insurance Calculators.
www.money-zine.com/Category/Insurance-Calculators/
Morningstar Tools.
    www.morningstar.com/Cover/Tools.html
Mortgages. www.mtgprofessor.com
Mutual Fund Calculator. http://www.sec.gov/investor/tools/mfcc/mfcc-int.htm
Social Security Benefit Calculator.
    www.ssa.gov/planners/calculators.htm
Yahoo Calculators. finance.yahoo.com/calculator/index
Yahoo! Insurance Calculators.
    finance.yahoo.com/insurance

Financial Planning

Christian

Crown Ministries. www.crown.org
Dave Ramsey. www.daveramsey.com
Focus on the Family. www.focusonthefamily.com
Ron Blue Business. www.ronblue.com and www.everydaysteward.com
Ron Blue Ministry. www.mastermoney.org

General

Best Places to Live. www.bestplaces.net
Bureau of Labor Statistics. www.bls.gov/cpi/home.htm and www.bls.gov/emp/emptab7.htm
Consumer Price Index. www.bls.gov/cpi/home.htm
Financial Designations. www.finra.org/designations/
Financial Trend Forecaster. www.fintrend.com/ftf/
Free Tax Filing. www.irs.gov/app/freeFile/welcome.jsp
Internal Revenue Service. www.irs.gov
Medical Information Report. www.mib.com
Microsoft Templates. www.microsoft.com
Public Personal Information Report.
    www.choicepoint.com
Salary.com. www.salary.com
SalaryExpert. www.salaryexpert.com
The Financial Forecast Center. www.forecasts.org/inflation.htm

U. S. Census Bureau. www.census.gov/population/www/socdemo/education/cps2008.html

Budgeting

Budgeting Worksheet. financialplan.about.com/cs/budgeting/l/blbudget.htm
Crosswalk.com. www.crosswalk.com
Online Envelopes. crown.mvelopes.com
The Finance Center.
    www.financecenter.com/products/calculators
You Need a Budget. www.youneedabudget.com

Giving

Charity Navigator. www.charitynavigator.com
Charity Watch. www.charitywatch.org
Evangelical Council for Financial Accountability.
    www.ecfa.org
GuideStar. www.guidestar.com
Ministry Watch. www.ministrywatch.com

Credit and Banking

Banking Information and Rates. www.bankrate.com
Bankruptcy Statistics. www.uscourts.gov/bnkrpctystats/bankruptcystats.htm
Credit Cards. www.cardweb.com
Credit Information. www.myfico.com
Credit Laws. www.fdic.gov/regulations/laws/rules/6500-200.html
Credit Pre-Screen Opt-Out. www.optoutprescreen.com
FDIC. www.fdic.gov
Find Free Checking. www.checkingfinder.com
Free Annual Credit Report. www.annualcreditreport.com
NCUA. www.ncua.gov

Investing

General

Austin Pryor. www.soundmindinvesting.com
Bloomberg. www.bloomberg.com
Buy Treasury Bonds. www.treasurydirect.gov
Financial Times. www.financialtimes.com
Forbe's. www.forbes.com
Fortune. www.fortune.com
Google Finance. www.google.com/finance
Kiplinger's. www.kiplinger.com
Money. www.money.com
Moody's. www.moodys.com
Morningstar. www.morningstar.com
Motley Fool. www.fool.com
Online Company Reports. www.edgar-online.com
Profitability Report. www.inc.com/keyword/nov08
Saving Bond Wizard. www.treasurydirect.gov/indiv/tools/tools_savingsbondwizard.htm
Securities and Exchange Commission. www.sec.gov

U. S. Treasury. www.publicdebt.treas.gov
Yahoo Finance. finance.yahoo.com

Stocks

American Stock Transfer and Trust. www.amstock.com
Bank of New York. www.stockbny.com
Barron's. www.barrons.com
BigCharts.com. www.bigcharts.com
Charles Schwab. www.schwab.com
Computershare. www.computershare.com
Dow Jones. www.dowjones.com
E-trade. www.etrade.com
Firstrade. www.firstrade.com
GuruFocus. http://www.gurufocus.com/news.
php?id=36158
Market Watch. www.marketwatch.com
Mellon Investor Services. www.melloninvestor.com
Merrill Lynch. www.ml.com
New York Stock Exchange. www.nyse.com
Smart Money. www.smartmoney.com
Standard & Poor's. www.standardandpoors.com
StockCharts.com. www.stockcharts.com
TD Ameritrade. www.tdameritrade.com
The Staton Institute. www.statoninstitute.com
Value Line. www.valueline.com
Wall Street Journal. www.wsj.com

Bonds

BondHeads.com. www.bondheads.com
BondKnwoledge.com. www.bondknowledge.com
BondMarkets.com. www.bondmarkets.com
BondPage.com. www.bondpage.com
BondTalk.com. www.bondtalk.com
BondWeek. www.bondweek.com
FMSbonds.com. www.fmsbonds.com
Harrisdirect. www.harrisdirect.com
Institutional Investor Journals. www.iijournals.com
Institutional Investor. www.institutionalinvestor.com
Select Information Exchange Company.
        www.stockfocus.com
The Bond Market Association.
        www.investinginbonds.com

Mutual Funds

Brill Mutual Funds Interactive. www.brill.com
Fidelity. www.fidelity.com
Investment Company Institute. www.ici.org
MSN Money Mutual Fund Screener. moneycentral.msn.
com/investor/finder/mffinder.asp
Mutual Fund Prospector. www.ericdany.com
Mutual Fund Research Newsletter. funds-newsletter.com
Mutualfunds.com. www.mutualfunds.com
Quicken Mutual Fund Screener.
        screen.yahoo.com/funds.html?quicken=2
Securities and Exchange Commission. www.sec.gov
Standards & Poor's. www.funds-sp.com

Vanguard. www.vanguard.com
Zack's. www.zacks.com

Insurance

AARP. assets.aarp.org/rgcenter/il/2006_13_ltci.pdf
AccuQuote. www.accuquote.com
Allstate Insurance. www.allstate.com
CNN Money Insurance. money.cnn.com/pf/insurance/
Geico Insurance. www.geico.com
HSA Insider. www.hsainsider.com
Insurance Information Institute. www.iii.org
Insure.com. www.insure.com
Insweb.com. www.insweb.com
LeadFusion. www.leadfusion.com
Life Insurance Wiz. www.lifeinsurancewiz.com
Long Term Care. http://www.fool.com/insurancecenter/
longterm/longterm01.htm
Medi-Share. www.biblicalhealthcare.com
Motley Fool. www.fool.com
National Highway Safety Institute.
        http://www.iihs.org/ratings/default.aspx
Progressive Insurance. www.progressive.com
Quicken Insurance. www.quickeninsurance.com
Samaritan Ministries. www.samaritanministries.org
State Auto Insurance Requirements.
        insure.com/auto/minimum.html
State Farm Insurance. www.statefarm.com
U.S. Treasury HSA Information.
        www.ustreas.gov/offices/public-affairs/hsa/
Yahoo! Insurance. insurance.yahoo.com

Shopping and Services

General

BizRate. www.bizrate.com
Consumer Reports. www.consumerreports.org
iStorez. www.istorez.com
MySimon. www.mysimon.com
NexTag. www.nextag.com
Price Grabber. www.pricegrabber.com
Price Protectr. www.priceprotectr.com
RefundPlease. www.refundplease.com

Cars

Auto Leasing Resource Center. www.leasetips.com
Auto Zone. www.autozone.com
Autocheck. www.autocheck.com
CarBuyingTips.com. www.carbuyingtips.com/lease.htm
CarFax. www.carfax.com
Cars.com. www.cars.com
CarSmart. www.carsmart.com
Consumer Guide. www.consumerguide.com
Edmunds. www.edmunds.com
Kelly Blue Book. www.kbb.com
LeaseCompare.com. www.leasecompare.com
LeaseGuide.com. www.leaseguide.com

National Automobile Dealers Association. www.nada.com
The Auto Channel. www.theautochannel.com
Trust My Mechanic.com. www.trustmymechanic.com

Home

Ace Hardware. www.ace.com
DIY Network. www.diynetwork.com
DoItYourself.com. www.doityourself.com
Domania. www.domania.com
Expert Village. www.expertvillage.com
HomeGain. www.homegain.com
Lowes. www.lowes.com
MonkeySee. www.monkeysee.com
Real Estate. www.realtor.com
Yahoo Real Estate. realestate.yahoo.com/re/homevalues/

Education

American Bar Association. www.abanet.org/legalservices/
sclaid/lrap/home.html
American Federation of Teachers.
        www.aft.org/tools4teachers/loan-forgiveness.htm
AmeriCorps. www.americorps.gov
Association of American Medical Schools. services.aamc.
org/fed_loan_pub/index.cfm
Equal Justice Works. www.equaljusticeworks.org/re-
sources/student-debt-relief/default
Federal Student Aid. studentaid.ed.gov/PORTALSWe-
bApp/students/english/childcare.jsp and
studentaid.ed.gov/PORTALSWebApp/students/english/
teachercancel.jsp
Health Resources and Services Administration.
        bhpr.hrsa.gov/nursing/loanrepay.htm
Kiplinger's. www.kiplinger.com/tools/colleges/
National Health Services Corps.
        nhsc.hrsa.gov/loanrepayment/
National Institute of Health. www.lrp.nih.gov
Peace Corps. www.peacecorps.gov
U. S. Military. www.military.com/education-home/
U. S. Office of Personnel Management.
        www.opm.gov/oca/pay/studentloan/
U.S. News. www.usnews.com

Computer

CompuForums. www.compuforums.com
MaximumPC. www.maximumpc.com
TechGuy. www.techguy.com

Vacation

Digsville. www.digsville.com
Home Exchange. www.homeexchange.com
HomeLink International. www.homelink.com
Intervac. www.intervac.com

Retirement and Estate Planning

AARP. www.aarp.org
CNN Money. money.cnn.com/retirement
Nolo. www.nolo.com

Index